Christ's Directives
on the Nature of True Worship
by Arthur Hildersham
with chapters by C. Matthew McMahon

Copyright Information

Table of Contents

Applying the
Regulative Principle
by C. Matthew McMahon, Ph.D., Th.D.

Many ministers today who are part of a reformed, or a reforming church, are often "horrified" at the *application* of the biblical *Regulative Principle of Worship* (RPW) because it becomes uncomfortable, or even dangerous in their church, to righteously hold to it. What do I mean by this? There must be a distinction made between three groups, 1) those who *say* they hold to the Regulative Principle, but don't. 2) Those who both hold to it and actually apply it rightly and biblically. 3) Those who hold to it, and *think* they apply it, but they apply it unbiblically. It is certainly possible to hold to the RPW and misuse it. But in trying to figure out what the truth is, should we react as *horrified* at the way God prescribes worship for his church, and should we react as horrified in the way that worship is applied in our church services? Should we be horrified when someone says, "Unless we do what God says, then we are idolaters"? *Certainly not.* Holding to the RPW marks us out as believers of God's word and true Christians!

First, most basically, let's set forth a definition of the RPW that is both consistent with the bible and rightly applied to worship, and with historic confessions. We do not want to fall liable to Christ's rebuke by being part of vain worship, which is *idolatry*. "But in vain they do worship me, teaching for doctrines the commandments of men," (Matt. 15:9). Though the early church certainly taught that worship is regulated by God, the RPW was given its classical and definitive statement in the Reformed confessions formulated in the 17th century. It is stated in the *1647 Westminster Confession of Faith*, 21:7:

> The light of nature showeth that there is a God, who hath lordship and sovereignty over all, is good, and doth good unto all, and is therefore to be feared, loved, praised, called upon, trusted in, and served, with all the heart, and with all the soul, and with all the might.[1] But the acceptable way of worshiping the true God is instituted by himself, and so limited by his own revealed will, that he may not be worshiped according to the imaginations and devices of men, or the suggestions of Satan, under any visible representation, or any other way not prescribed in the Holy Scripture.[2]

To make this even simpler, true worship is commanded only by God; false worship is anything not commanded. That's quite simple overall. God *alone* determines the manner in which sinners may approach him. It should be seen as appropriate that *the house of God* be ordered by God's rules. It should be seen as appropriate that God's *people* are to be ordered by God's rules. It should be seen as appropriate that *worship to Christ*, that which shows

---

[1] Romans 1:20; Psalm 19:1-4a; 50:6; 86:8-10; 89:5-7; 95:1-6; 97:6; 104:1-35; 145:9-12; Acts 14:17; Deut. 6:4-5.
[2] Deut. 4:15-20; 12:32; Matt. 4:9-10; 15:9; Acts 17:23-25; Exod. 20:4-6; John 4:23-24; Col. 2:18-23.

reverence, piety, love, desire, and joy in God to Christ, be structured and ordered according to *God's word* and *His biblical principles lying therein.* Who would disagree with this? Who would be *horrified* at this? Today...many, in fact, *most ministers are horrified at this.*

Worship for the Christian should be an expression of God's heart back to God. Christians ought to reflect back to God how wonderful and most blessed he is. Now here is the rub: it is *impossible* to worship God by human invention. It is *impossible* to worship God by human ingenuity. It is *impossible* to worship God in an atmosphere that has not been structured and ordered by God and his word. Take that to heart – *it is impossible to do it, regardless of how sincere a person may be.* It may very well be that people are in a worship service doing something *they think* is worship to God, when it is in fact, not worship. The RPW, which is found in Scripture and expressed clearly by all the good Reformers, as well as in its climactic expression by the Puritans, even the early church, should not be placed by the way side because our contemporary culture and church are *horrified* when it is applied rightly in our church services.

Some people will say that inconclusive ideas on the RPW are the very reason why there are so many denominations and so many views. People just *cannot* agree. Was that Christ's position and conclusion? Hold that thought for a moment. Consider, for example:

> Some wear head coverings in the public worship service, others don't.
> Some use wine for the Lord's Supper, others don't.

Some have an evening worship service, others don't.

Some baptize only adults who have an audible profession of faith, others don't.

Some use instruments in worship, others don't.

Some people believe that just so long as a person *feels* convicted about what they believe, even if these are brilliant and godly people who want to properly interpret the Bible, well, they come to "different conclusions" and it's *alright*, so long as *you have a peace about it.* Where in the bible is anything remotely even close to this taught? And yet, ministers *think* this way all the time, and church congregations *act* this way all the time. Would this apply also to heretics so long as they are sincere in *their* interpretation of Scripture? In this, people believe that the arguments surrounding the RPW can go *on and on.* And they think, at the end of the day, a person simply has to "pick what you want to practice and have peace with it." That kind of thinking from professing Christians is a grand mistake. It is, in fact, a *rejection* of the RPW, not an avowed upholding of it before God. Such is a non-reformed position, and I may add, a very unbiblical one. In fact, as you will see in this work by Arthur Hildersham, he calls it *the worship of the devil.* Do you think that language is too strong?

Consider the indented statements given above in a different light. Know, that each statement, even according to the law of plain logic, one is right and one is wrong. One is biblical, one is idolatry as it pertains to worship. *They both cannot be right.* For example, throughout recent years there have been a whole host of opinions on how the Lord's Supper works, and the use of wine or grape juice greatly due to the temperance movement in the early 1900s. One church says, "wine" is the element according to the RPW for the Lord's Supper and another says, "no, grape juice is" *per* the same RPW. Can they *both* be right? Lest I be rebuked for saying, *no*, we must at least start thinking rightly, and at the very least say *one is wrong, and one is right, one is prescribed by God and one is not.* Which one? That doesn't matter at this point. In all fairness, it could be that *both* positions are wrong. Maybe God wants his people to use orange juice? Regardless of conjecture, they cannot *both* be right. *Sorry.* But it is up to the church to figure out which one is right and which one is wrong, or, what God prescribes, and why, *and do that.* And when we do figure it out, it's up to us to *obey* what God prescribes. I don't think that's *horrifying*, although many ministers certainly think so because it leads them into compromising places with their church and denomination *that they would rather ignore.*

I'm not arguing here *for* or *against* any of those statements indented in the paragraph above. All I am saying is that a person cannot leave conclusions in the realm of "just be at peace with what you like and, O well, there it is," without knowing whether they are in fact standing on the truth of the bible or not. They have to be at least willing to say, "they both can't be true." One *has* to be wrong. At that point, they should be thoroughly turning to both Scripture, and then even how that particular doctrine might fall out in the realm of historical theology (what did others believe on this and why in church history?).

None of those statements about doing one thing or another are matter of *circumstance*. They are all rooted in the *elements* of worship and the RPW. In other words, if we were discussing the color of the Psalter that we use, a red, blue or black book cover, that is a circumstantial. The color really doesn't matter in the grand scheme of spiritual worship *in any way*. What does matter are the *elements* of worship: those prescriptions God commands that we are to follow without changing them or detracting from them or adding to them.

Just read the same indented statements in a different way. This should help clear up the point:

> If God prescribed head coverings in public worship, and I don't instruct on wearing them, or my church does not use them, it's idolatry.
> If God prescribed wine for the supper, and I don't use it, it's idolatry.
> If God prescribed me to baptize only people who make a profession, and I don't do that, it's idolatry.
> If God prescribed me to use musical instruments in worship, and I don't, it's idolatry.

If I offer strange fire on the altar, (see Lev. 10:1-3), and God didn't prescribe it, am I in and under the same condemnation as Nadab and Abihu as a minister?[3] Is God

---

[3] See Jeremiah Burroughs on that in his work, *Gospel Worship*, published by Puritan Publications on Leviticus 10:3.

"in" those things he doesn't prescribe? No, in fact, *he isn't.* God himself tells us that *he isn't.* "He said furthermore unto me, Son of man, seest thou what they do? even the great abominations that the house of Israel committeth here, that I should *go far off* from my sanctuary?" (Ezek. 8:6). God says that *idolatry drives him out of the sanctuary.*

God never says that you can just chalk up your worship to whatever you feel like. He never says anything remotely like that in Scripture, *ever.* He never gives anyone the right to be wrong about his mind. We must make sure that we "pick" at the mind of God correctly in Scripture (where his mind is fully revealed for life and godliness) even among topics we deem difficult to understand; but most especially in his *worship.* Otherwise, as Hildersham shows, we worship devils instead of God.

God consistently, and continually instructs his people to do what he commands, and consistently, and continually punishes idolatry. With so many divisions today on the church at large, this ought to be causing every church in every place to fall down on their faces in collective prayer to discern God's will rightly according to Scripture. Does not the Apostle Peter say, "...judgment must begin at the house of God," (1 Peter 4:17)?

Also consider that God never, ever positively blesses anything he does not prescribe in worship, which is why, across the board, for every professing Christian everywhere, they better be sure their position of worship (or any biblical foundation for that matter) is *God's position.* They must never be, in fact, doing whatever they "deem" or "think" or "want" in worship from some personal position of "I hope I'm right." To overthrow

God's prescribed rule of worship, even by accident, is in fact vain and idolatrous, which God calls spiritual adultery.[4]

We should never settle only in "hoping" we have things right in worship to the living God. "It is a fearful thing to fall into the hands of the living God," (Heb. 10:31). In John 4, Christ says that the Father seeks worshippers who worship him in spirit and truth, (the substance of this very treatise by Hildersham). We ought to *strictly know what that means*. We ought to have that biblically straight. Otherwise, if we commit idolatry against him, we have a myriad of Scriptures that specifically tell us that God will 1) be driven from the sanctuary, and 2) punish the wickedness of our idolatry.

It is important that you see I am not arguing for one position over another here. I'm arguing that we need to be sure we are *right*, or otherwise, *we are idolaters* regardless of how sincere we are if we are doing that which is wrong. There is no comfortable middle ground, and sincerity or earnestness is not the foundation on which truth is bred. And if we are idolaters, then God is *not* in that worship, and will not bless that worship regardless of how we *feel* about it. He detests it and despises it regardless of what *we might think*. We can learn a great amount of insight into this by just considering what God says to Ephraim in matters of mixed or idolatrous worship in the book of Hosea alone. Consider these Scriptures:

---

[4] Jer. 3:2, 5:7; Ezek. 16:15-16, 32-33; Hos. 1:2, 4:13-14.

"Ephraim, he hath mixed himself among the people; Ephraim is a cake not turned," (Hos. 7:8).

"Ephraim is joined to idols: let him alone. Their drink is sour: they have committed whoredom continually," (Hos. 4:17-18).

There are so many warnings against spiritual adultery and idolatry, that we cannot afford being comfortable with so many divisions in the contemporary church. God tells Ephraim, his church, that they are a *cake not turned*, burned on one side and raw on the other, good for nothing in their idolatrous worship but to be thrown out. He even goes so far to tell Hosea that Ephraim ought to be left alone, because of the very fact that she is *joined to idolatry*. Even the means of grace are no longer useful to them. To remain on point, the RPW itself doesn't allow for a middle view on any part of worship. It is a principle, regulated by God, that we conform to, *i.e.* we are to do what God says and nothing else of any kind in any way.

Now, someone might say that a "distinction needs to be made between an Ephraim who knowingly or intentionally engages in false worship, or the worship of the true God in false ways, and, an Ephraim who, according to his understanding of the Scriptures (though he may be wrong), or out of ignorance, who has taken up a form of worshipping God in a way not commanded, though in earnest." However, this is a false dichotomy. Let me explain what I mean.

If Ephraim decides that they want to engage in something that God has not prescribed in worship, and they do it willfully and obstinately as idolatry, God hates that. Since God has not prescribed it, we know that everything not prescribed *he hates*. He will not bless idolatry. That seems straight forward. Now, consider the other hand, if Ephraim, unknowing (not obstinately), comes to commit idolatry *by accident*, does God accept this? Does Christ cover idolatry with his blood *as idolatry?* Does he give *idolatry a pass?* Not at all, in fact, *never*. What is missing in this objection, is considering *the third option.*

Consider, what if Ephraim comes to worship God in order to do all that God prescribes, but does it poorly and imperfectly as fallen but redeemed sinners; does God accept that? Yes, but only through Jesus Christ. In a certain light, all Christians who hold and apply the RPW are sinful worshippers. Our worship to God is only ever accepted as our robes are dipped in his blood.[5] Our worship is only received by God and blessed as we come doing what God commands, though imperfect, as we bring Jesus Christ to that worship. Such worship is *not* idolatry. Such worship is merely tainted with sin, imperfect, and covered by the Savior's redeeming blood on our behalf. Such worship is motioned in us to give to God all the glory, by the Spirit. We ought, in all our duties, to bring Christ to them. Without doing that, God will not accept us. We are accepted, "in the Beloved," and in no other way.[6] Ultimately, what will God give earnest Ephraim who worships as God prescribes, but imperfectly, tainted with sin? Will God be judgmental? Will he see imperfect worship, worship that he

---

[5] "These are they which came out of great tribulation, and have washed their robes, and made them white in the blood of the Lamb," (Rev. 7:14).
[6] "To the praise of the glory of his grace, wherein he hath made us accepted in the beloved," (Eph. 1:6).

prescribes, idolatrous? Or will he be *merciful in Christ?* God will always *bless* everything offered up to him as it is offered and done in the work of Christ *as prescribed by his word.* In contrast, he will *never* bless anything that he has not prescribed, even if it is done by a Christian who is earnest in their *idolatry.*

I don't know any orthodox reformed writer or preacher in the last 500 years of the church, that would disagree with all that; as a matter of fact, I don't know of any early church fathers that would disagree with that principal overall. Yet, still, ministers in the church *today* are horrified at these kinds of statements. Why would so many be *horrified* at such ideas unless the practical application of where the RPW leads them *horrifies them?* Maybe they are misunderstanding the RPW. Or maybe they don't like where the RPW takes them practically? Or maybe the RPW, taken to its end, is too difficult for their ministry, or might even rob them of their ministry, even in the church where they currently minister, because the people won't like what they are saying about worship. An orthodox respectable minister told me after discussing this topic years ago with them by email, and said, "If I start believing that application of the RPW then I'll be booted out of my church, and then, how will I feed my family?" I think this is often at the heart of those who might be *horrified* by the RPW.

With that said, don't be *horrified* by this little book by Arthur Hildersham, regardless of who you are. The RPW, explained in this volume by Hildersham, *will be horrifying* to those who leave worship in the "just do whatever you have peace with and leave it at that", point of view. In contrast to those people, all of the good teachers of the church say the same thing, as well as most of the reformers and the Puritans after them, as also the historic confessions. God's worship *never* changes. Why? Because 1) God never changes, and 2) because the Bible never changes, which is God's will. God's character and his will are forever the same.

Hildersham on worship, now, still says *same thing* that was said in his day, and what Jesus taught the woman at the well two thousand years ago. At the end of the day one must not simply pick what they want to practice and earnestly might have peace with it. Hildersham will vividly demonstrate from John 4, from Christ's directives, that one position is right and one is wrong. One is biblical, one is idolatry. And there is no peace with God in idolatrous worship, for earnest idolatry is never blessed by God.

In the Grace of Christ and for his glory,
C. Matthew McMahon, Ph.D., Th.D.
September, 2019
From my study.

Meet Arthur Hildersham

Edited by C. Matthew McMahon

Arthur Hildersham, A. M., (1563-1631)[7] was a celebrated divine descended from the royal family.[8] This divine being so honorably descended,[9] was born at Stechworth in Cambridgeshire on October 6, 1563, and educated in Christ's college, Cambridge. His parents were zealous papists, and he was brought up in all the errors and superstitions of popery, and taught to repeat his prayers in Latin. During his stay at the university, he embraced the protestant religion, and was highly esteemed on account of his learning, piety, affability, and

---

[7] Taken from Thomas Brooks', *Lives of the Puritans*, Volume 2.

[8] The famous Cardinal Poole was his great uncle. He was the son of Mr. Thomas Hildersham, a gentleman of an ancient family, and Ann Poole his second wife. See Mather's *Hist, of New. Eng.* b. iii. p. 181.

[9] Mrs. Hildersham was daughter to Sir Jeffery Poole, the fourth son of Sir Richard Poole, a German cousin to King Henry VII. Margaret, countess of Salisbury, the wife of Sir Richard Poole, and grandmother to Mr. Hildersham, was the daughter of George duke of Clarence (second brother to King Edward IV.) and Isabella, elder daughter and co-heir of Richard earl of Warwick and Salisbury.

inoffensive and witty conversation. His father no sooner knew of the change in his religious sentiments, that he took him from the university, and resolved to send him to Rome, with a view to have him reclaimed, in order to become a priest. Young Hildersham, however, was fixed in his protestant principles, and refused to go; for which his father cast him off and disinherited him. In this way, he whom God had appointed to be a great sufferer in his cause, began to bear the yoke in his youth by forsaking parents, friends, and all earthly comforts, and the certain prospect of worldly advancement, for the sake of Christ and the testimony of a good conscience.

In this forlorn situation, God, *who comforteth his people in all their tribulations,* comforted Mr. Hildersham, through the kind assistance of Mr. John Ireton, then of Cambridge, but afterwards rector of Kegworth in Leicestershire. This gentleman providentially meeting him in London, said to him, "Arthur, why art thou so long from thy books, losing so much time?" "Alas, sir," said he, "I shall go no more to Cambridge;" and then gave him a particular account of his unhappy condition. "Well," said Mr. Ireton, "be not discouraged. Thou hast a noble kinsman, whom I will acquaint with thy case; and I doubt not that he will provide for thee." He accordingly laid his distressed situation before Henry earl of Huntingdon, lord president of the north, whose mother and Mr. Hildersham's mother were his brother's children. The noble earl gladly embraced this opportunity of showing his kindness and generosity. He warmly espoused his cause, sent him again to the university, and afforded him his liberal support.

Hildersham entered his public ministerial function; but he presently received a sudden check, and was convened before the high commission, suspended from his ministry, and deprived of his fellowship, chiefly for preaching occasionally before he took orders. This was done by the particular instigation of Archbishop Whitgift, who commanded him to make a public recantation, and required him to enter into bonds to appear again on a certain day before the high commission, if he presumed to refuse. The form of his recantation, dated January 10, 1588, was the following:

"I confess that I have rashly and indiscreetly taken upon me to preach, not being licensed, nor admitted into holy orders, contrary to the orders of the church of England; contrary to the example of antiquity; and contrary to the direction of the apostle in the Acts: whereby I have given great and just offence to many; and the more, because I have uttered in my sermons certain impertinent, and very unfit speeches for the auditory, as moving their minds to discontent with the state, rather than tending to of godly edification. For which my presumption and indiscretion, I am very heartily sorry, and desire you to bear witness of this my confession, and acknowledging my said offences."[10]

It is extremely doubtful whether Mr. Hildersham ever recanted; for he was, previous to the above date,

---

[10] Baker's *MS. Colleg.* vol. ii. p. 445. MS. Register, p. 82.

called from the university by the Earl of Huntingdon, and appointed to preach at Ashby-de-la-Zouch in Leicestershire. In this situation he continued to the end of his days, though not without frequent molestations and interruptions. He was a man of great piety, learning, charity, and very peaceable, and one who loved all pious and learned men, whatever might be their opinions of the discipline and ceremonies. Although he was a minister in the established church, and so far opposed a total separation from it, that he was called *the hammer of schismatics,* yet "he was," says Mr. Clark, "always, from his first entrance into the ministry, a resolved and conscientious nonconformist." He labored hard, in concert with his brethren, to obtain a more pure reformation of the national church. His honest and decided attachment to what he considered to be the truth, exposed him to all those oppressions and cruelties with which he was exercised. He was frequently silenced from his ministry, and treated in many other respects with the utmost barbarity; notwithstanding which he usually attended upon the prayers, sermons, and sacraments, at the established church. All his excellent endowments were insufficient to screen him from the tyrannical proceedings of the ruling ecclesiastics.

In the year 1590 he married the daughter of Mr. Barfoot of Lamborn-hall in Essex. She was his constant companion in all his tribulations, and an excellent comforter under his numerous and painful sufferings. During the first year of his marriage, his faith and patience were put to the trial. He was convened before the high commission, suspended from his ministry, and obliged to enter into bonds, prohibiting him from attending upon the duties of his ministry in any part of England. The year following, he was partially restored, but still forbidden to preach at any place south of the river Trent.[11] This prohibition utterly excluded him from laboring among his beloved people at Ashby. But this restraint was afterwards taken away, when he returned to his stated ministerial charge at that place.

His name was often honorably mentioned in the presence of Queen Elizabeth. On these occasions she used to describe him as cousin Hildersham. By her majesty's favor, he was released from the ecclesiastical censure.

During the accession of King James, numerous petitions were presented to his majesty and the parliament, for a further reformation of the church. Mr. Hildersham, being a leading person among the puritans, and universally beloved by all the enemies of superstition and oppression, was appointed, with several of his brethren, to present these petitions, and, if required, to defend them by disputation. At the Hampton-court conference, our worthy divine, together with Mr. Stephen Egerton of London, and Mr. Edward Fleetwood of Lancashire, presented a number of requests to his majesty, earnestly desiring a further reformation in ecclesiastical matters.

It was impossible for Mr. Hildersham to act in this public capacity without being particularly noticed. The eyes of the jealous prelates were fixed upon him. Therefore, in the year 1605, he was silenced by the Bishop of Lincoln for nonconformity. Afterwards, he obtained some favor from the Bishop of Lichfield and Coventry,

---

[11] MS. *Chronology*, Vol. iii. A. D. 1631. p. 8.

who allowed him to preach occasionally in his diocese, particularly at the two famous associations at Repton in Derbyshire, and Burton-upon-Trent in Staffordshire. These associations were designed for private conference among the ministers, and the public ministry of the word. They were the means of doing unspeakable good to both ministers and people; and Mr. Hildersham was a chief promoter of them for many years. His fame, indeed, was so great in those parts, that for many years after, when any one became remarkable for true piety, he was sure to be stigmatized as "one of Hildersham's old puritans."

It was after his restoration at this time that he entered upon his "Lectures on John 4," which continued every Tuesday for upwards of two years.

These lectures were afterwards published, in 1628, and dedicated to Henry earl of Huntingdon, who attended them, when preached in Ashby church, and whose uncle and grandfather had been the author's worthy patrons. Dr. Williams says, "that these lectures discover the author to be a sound divine, an admirable textuary, a profoundly experienced Christian, and an excellent teacher."[12]

He had numerous interruptions and oppressions to his ministry. Mr. Hildersham had to pass through the fire of persecution many times. Yet, he continued preaching until December 27th 1631 when he preached his last sermon.[13]

In this way, our pious and learned divine knew by painful experience the truth of that doctrine which he delivered to the people. "Every faithful minister," he says,

---

[12] *Christian Preacher*, p. 435.
[13] Clark's *Lives*, p. 122.

"who laboreth to win souls to God, shall be sure to be rewarded, how ill soever an unthankful world may reward him. If we judge by sense and reason, we shall hardly be able to conceive how it can be true; for no kind of men ever seems to be more neglected of God in this life, than faithful ministers. In all ages these men have been in much trouble, and their enemies have prevailed against them and that oftentimes even unto death. But," he says, "if with a special care to provide for faithful ministers; and that one have such promises of protection and deliverance from trouble. If it please the Lord to let his ministers suffer, it is," he says, "either because their testimony is finished; or because God will receive more honor by their suffering and constant confession of his truth, than by their peace. As the apostle says of his own troubles, "would, brethren, ye should understand, that the things which have happened unto me, have fallen out rather unto the furtherance of the gospel."

This excellent servant of Christ discovered in his last sickness very becoming submission to the will of God. His conversation was spiritual, holy, and heavenly. He gave solemn charge to his son, to take heed unto the flock of Christ; and on the Lord's Day, while his son was at prayer with him, he closed his eyes in peace, and entered upon the joy of his Lord, March 4, 1631, aged sixty-eight years.

Mr. Hildersham preached at Ashby upwards of forty-three years, excepting the intervals of his suspension for nonconformity. He was a pious, learned, and useful preacher. Fuller describes him "a worthy divine, and a just and upright man," but has incorrectly classed him among the fellows and learned writers of

Christ's college, Cambridge.[14] Echard describes him "a great and shining light of the puritan party," and observes, "that he was justly celebrated for his singular learning and piety."[15] He was a divine of great moderation, and of a most amiable Christian spirit. He used to say, "that he never heard any faithful preacher of the gospel, however mean his talents might be, but he could discover some gift in him that was wanting in himself, and could receive some profit from his preaching."

His works:

In addition to his lectures on John 4 and Psalm 51 (which are enormous), Mr. Hildersham was author of "Lectures on Psalm 35," published in 1632; and "A Treatise on the Lord's Supper." Of this work, Mr. John Cotton says, "Those questions and answers furnish a Christian with a more proper view of that spiritual duty, than any other book in any language, that I know, in so small a compass."

---

[14] Fuller's *Worthies*, part i. p. 159.—Hist, of Cam. p. 92.
[15] Echard in *Hist, of Eng.* vol. ii. p. 98.

Notation on
the Abridged Version
by C. Matthew McMahon

This work is an abridged version of Hildersham's commentary on the fourth chapter of John. It was originally titled "108 lectures upon the fourth of John," published in 1632. The original work spans almost 1000 pages, and comprised 108 "lectures" or really *sermons*, which Hildersham preached to a congregation in Ashby-Delazouch in Leicester-shire. It went through various editions, and the second edition, from which this treatise is drawn, was updated by Hildersham himself and expanded. It was so lengthy that the second edition housed an index of key words and Scriptures that ran, of itself, 43 pages.

The introduction to the "Godly Reader" by the original publisher, confessed that he knew there was a great amount of godly material in the pages, but could not rightly edit the work down to a reasonable size and thought it best, for his purposes, to transcribe the whole work at the time. He says, "But in this book (to tell you what I find) I find such variety of choice matter running throughout every vein of each discourse handled in it, and carried along with such strength of sound and deep judgment, and with such life and power of a heavenly Spirit, and with it expressed in such pithy and pregnant words of wisdom, that I did not know what to select, and what to omit, unless I should have transcribed the whole book."

It may be that at a later time a publisher will find the task of transcribing the whole work profitable. No doubt, Hildersham has much good to say. But, for now, this abridged version has been prayerfully edited to its current size so that not only will readers have a chance to read a manageable book on worship by this exemplary puritan, but also that they might focus on the most proper lectures concerning *Christ's Directives on the Nature of True Worship.*

CHAPTER 1:
THE WHOLE MAN IN WORSHIP

"Ye worship ye know not what: we know what we worship: for salvation is of the Jews. But the hour cometh, and now is, when the true worshippers shall worship the Father in spirit and in truth: for the Father seeketh such to worship him. God is a Spirit: and they that worship him must worship him in spirit and in truth," (John 4:22-24).

In contemplating the text, the question the Samaritan woman posed to Christ concerns true worship; about the most public and solemn worship of God. Now the word that the Evangelist uses to express this worship that he speaks of, is προσκυνοῦντας (John 4:20), which signifies to *adore*, so that the words may be plainly and fitly translated in this way, "Our Fathers adored in this mountain," *etc.* Now, *adoration* (to speak properly of it) is an outward and bodily worship, when by some reverent gesture of the body, we testify the inward reverence, and subjection of the heart. And the Greek word which the Evangelist uses here (in his primitive sense) signifies to *give a kiss unto another*, and it is taken from a custom they had in old times, to testify the reverence and subjection they bore to any, by giving them a kiss. So soon as Samuel had anointed Saul to be King to testify his homage to him, he gives him a kiss, (1 Sam. 10:1). When the Lord would describe his people that had not given religious worship to Baal, he calls them such as had not *bowed their knee to him, nor give him a kiss* with their mouths, (1 Kings 19:18). And when the Prophet would exhort the great men of the world to worship Christ, and to acknowledge him as their Lord and King, he bids them *kiss the Son* least he be angry, (Psalm 2:12).

Now the thing that we are first of all to observe at this time is, that the true worship of God is called *adoration.* In the four verses following Christ calls all that perform any true worship to God, such as do *adore* him. So, the whole worship where the Gentiles should be called, is signified under this phrase, Isaiah 45:23, "unto me every knee shall bow." And in this verse, you see that those which performed public and solemn worship to God in his temple, are said "to adore him," (Acts 8:27). The Eunuch is said to have come to Jerusalem to *adore,* (Acts 24:11). Paul says of himself, he came to Jerusalem to *adore.* And from here we have this to learn for our instruction: that no man can perform any part of God's worship well, (especially of his public and solemn worship) without some signification of his reverence and subjection to God, even in the outward gesture and behavior of his body. It is true, 1. That this is not enough, for the most chief part of God's service. But when with the soul we worship him, for in this way a hypocrite may go very far in the use of his body. 2. It is a high degree of contempt done to God when we think it is enough to give him the knee, if the heart does not bow to him, if we do not serve him with the heart. It is as the offering of the blind, lame and sick in sacrifice, of which the Lord says in Mal. 1:8, "is that not evil? offer it to thy prince," *etc.* Yet the service of the body is also necessary, and a part of God's worship. The chief worship we perform to God is done not with the body, but with the soul and spirit; as we shall hear when we come to speak of the 23ʳᵈ verse of this chapter. It is there in true reverence and subjection we bow our hearts to him, to walk in his ways, and do whatever reverence we can make show of with our bodies. But if our hearts do not bow with us to him, it is but abominable hypocrisy in the sight of God. But yet, be mindful that it is *not sufficient* to worship God only with our souls and hearts, if in every part of his worship we do not also adore, and give bodily worship to him. By the reverent behavior of our body, we testify of the inward submission and reverence of our hearts to him, though our souls in it are full of reverence and devotion. If we don't add our bodies to our heart, we serve him by *halves*, and our service cannot be acceptable to him.

You shall hear this confirmed to you by the examples of God's servants that are commended to us by the Holy Spirit. See the conscience God's people have made of this in all the parts of God's worship. Observe it in five points.

1. In prayer, when they even in private have prayed to God, they have been accustomed to kneel. For this we have the example of Daniel in 6:10, and of our Savior himself in Luke 22:41.

2. When they have given thanks (though but in private) they have used adoration. When Abraham's servant perceived that God had prospered his journey so far forth as to bring him and guide him safely to Bethuell's house, presently he lifted up his heart in thankfulness to God, yet did not think that was enough, but Gen. 24:26, the man *bowed himself and worshipped the Lord*. And as his

success increased, so his thankfulness to God increased, and so did the outward reverence of his body also increase, (verse 52). When Abraham's servant heard them give consent that Rebecca might go with them, then he bowed himself to the very earth to the Lord. So, Jacob giving thanks to God, and unable through weakness to stand or kneel, yet in token of reverence, raised himself up to his bed's head, and being not able through feebleness to sit upright, he leaned, and bore himself on his staff, and so adored God, (Gen. 47:31; Heb. 11:21). See the conscience this good old man made of this duty, and the pains he took in it.

3. When they have taken an oath, they have been accustomed to use such gestures of their body as might stir up reverence in their hearts, (Gen. 14:22). Abraham when he swore, he *lifted up his hand to the Lord*, the most high Possessor of heaven and earth.

4. When a message has been brought to them immediately from the Lord, they have been accustomed in token of their reverence, to rise and stand up. Judges 3:20, when Ehud told Eglon that he had a message from God to him, presently Eglon rose out of his throne, though he was a wicked man. Yet, this (without a doubt) he had learned from the custom and practice of God's people. So, Balaam likewise required Balaak the King to do. Num. 23:18, "Rise up Balaak and hear." Neh. 8:5, when Ezra opened the book of the Law to read, all the people *stood up*. "Rise up ye women that be at ease (the Lord says)," (Isaiah. 32:9), "hear my voice," alluding (without a doubt) in that speech to the holy custom used among God's people at the first intimation given to them of a message from God.

5. Lastly in the public, and solemn worship of God especially, they have held themselves bound to show this outward reverence. In Psalm 29:1-2 the Psalmist calls on great men to give to God *the glory due to his name*, and tells them how they may do that, "adore him, bow yourselves to him in his glorious Sanctuary." So also see Psalm 95:6 and make note of how many words the Prophet used to persuade to this, when he calls men to public worship. "Come, let us adore, and fall down, and kneel, before the Lord our maker." Therefore, the reverence to be done in God's public worship, is made a chief means to preserve religion, and coupled with the observation of the Sabbath, (Lev. 19:30 and 26:2). "Ye shall keep my Sabbaths, and reverence my sanctuary."

The reasons of this *doctrine* are of two sorts. There is some concern of the outward reverence to be used, in all the parts of God's worship, whether private, or public; some peculiarly concern the public and solemn worship of God.

1. This kind of humility befits everyone, even the greatest person to show when he has to come before God. See this in David's speech to Michal, 2 Sam. 6:20, 22, when he "danced before the ark she scoffed at him," he answers, "it was before the Lord," and adds, "I will be more vile, and I shall lose no honor by it." It is no disparagement for the greatest to debase and humble himself into the very dust before the Lord. No, we can never be humbled enough. "Behold now (Abraham says in Gen. 18:27), "I have taken upon me to speak unto the Lord which am but dust and ashes," and indeed who are we (*even the best of us*) that we should presume to speak unto God, or to appear before him. It becomes all men to cast

down their crowns before him, as the 24 elders did in Rev. 4:10. Yes, the holy angels (in Isaiah 6:2) "cover" their faces in his presence. We can do no service that is pleasing to him, unless it proceeds from a heart humbled in the sense of his high majesty, and our own vileness. Psalm 2:11, "Serve the Lord with fear." Micah 6:6, "Wherewith shall I come before the Lord, and bow myself before the high God." Eccl. 5:1, "Be not rash with thy mouth, neither let thine heart be hasty to utter a matter before God, for God is in the heavens and thou in the earth," *etc.*

2. Our bodies are the Lord's as well as our souls, and therefore he will be served also with the body. They are his by right of creation, redemption, and sanctification. The apostle gives this reason, "ye are bought with a price, therefore glorify God in your body and in your spirit which are God's," (1 Cor. 6:20).

3. That the humility and reverent gesture of the body may help to humble and work reverence in the heart. Our hearts are profane, and stand in need of all good outward helps, to stir up devotion in them. That is a chief reason why it was used both by Daniel (6:10) and Christ (Luke 22:41), in secret prayer, and if they needed to do so, how much more do we?

4. We do this to profess and testify the humility of the heart, and reverence of the soul. Therefore, this is put for the whole profession of our homage and obedience to God. "Unto me every knee shall bow," (Isaiah 45:23). Because in the matter of God's service, hypocrites are accustomed to pretend. They have as good hearts as the best. But the Lord is accustomed also to call so often for the service of the body, "Let not sin reign in your mortal

body," (Romans 6:12) and, "present your body as a living sacrifice, holy, acceptable unto God," (Romans 12:1), and, "glorify God in your body," (1 Cor. 6:20).

The reasons of that outward reverence that is to be used specially in the public and solemn worship of God, are three.

1. The presence of God's people. There is a reverence due from the greatest Prince to the meanest of God's servants, his brother must not seem vile to him, no not then when by any fault he has made himself worthy of punishment, (Deut. 25:3; Matt. 18:10). See that "ye despise not" one of these little ones. But specially to the congregation of God's people, when they are assembled to serve him, they should be seen and treated in such a manner. This reason the Apostle gives against certain abuses in the congregation of Corinth, (1 Cor. 11:22), "have ye not houses to eat and drink in," (he might have said, if he had lived among us, to sleep in, to talk, and laugh in) "despise ye the Church of God."

2. The presence of the holy angels, which as they have a charge from God to minister and do service to his people, (Heb. 1:15), and to pitch their tents about them, (Psalm 34:7), so they do so especially at that time when men are assembled together to serve the Lord. This was given as a figure or type to God's people under the Law. The curtains that the Tabernacle was made of, were full of cherubim, (Exod. 26:1). So were the walls of Solomon's temple round about, (1 Kings 6:29), to typify the presence and attendance of the holy angels on the whole church and body of God's people for their protection and safety, as at all other times, and in all other places. This is especially done in their church assemblies. This reason

the Apostle gives, why women should have modest attire in the congregation, (1 Cor. 11:10), is that the woman ought to have a sign on her head because of the angels.

3. The presence of the Lord himself, who though he is everywhere, (*cf.* Jer. 23:24, "Do not I fill heaven and earth saith the Lord," Acts 7:48, "The most high dwelleth not in Temples made with hands,") yet is he in a special way present in the congregation of his people, as is evident by those two promises made by our blessed Savior, Matt. 18:20 and 28:20. In this respect the public worship of God is called *the face and presence of God*, Psalm 105:4 and 42:2. And Cain, because of his murder, was deprived of the benefit of God's public worship, complains he should now be *hid from his face*, (Gen. 4. 14). That is the reason of David's desire, to dwell in the house of the Lord "all the days of his life," (Psalm 27:4). That I may say to, "behold the beauty of the Lord." And Psalm 48:9, "We wait for thy loving kindness O Lord in the midst of thy Temple." The place of God's public worship under the Law, is called "the glorious Sanctuary," (Psalm 26:2), because the glory of the Lord sensibly appeared in the tabernacle, (Exod. 40:34), and the temple, (1 Kings 8:10). And the assemblies of God's people now may as well be called *glorious*, because the glory of the Lord appears also in them, though not so sensibly, yet no less comfortably and effectually. This is plain by that comparison the Apostle makes between that ministry and worship of God that was under the Law and this that is under the Gospel, which he preferred (for glory and excellence) far above the other, (2 Cor. 3:8-9, 11).

CHAPTER 2:
REVERENT WORSHIP

The *use* that is to be made of rightly employing the heart and body in solemn worship, is: 1. For exhortation. 2. For reproof.

1. To exhort all men that they would learn to carry themselves reverently, in all the parts of God's worship and service, especially in his public worship. And that you may learn this better, I will give you certain rules out of God's word for your direction in this case. And these rules shall be of three sorts. 1. Such as belong in common to the whole worship of God. 2. Such as concern the public worship of God in general. 3. Such as are particular, and concern the several parts of that worship we do to God in the public assemblies.

And of those rules that are common to the whole worship of God, this is the first.

1. We are not bound to use all the same gestures in God's worship now, which we read in Scripture were of use among God's people, but such as by which in the country where we live, men are accustomed to express their reverence to their superiors. For this we find was the rule the faithful have followed in all ages. We read that Joshua, and the Elders of Israel, when they had received the foil at the siege of Ai, and came before the Ark of the Lord to pray, they "rent their clothes and put dust upon their heads," (Joshua 7:6). And when Hezekiah came into the house of the Lord to pray at that time when Senacharib besieged Jerusalem, rent his clothes and put on sackcloth, (Isaiah 37:1). Now none of these ceremonies

and fashions were peculiar to God's worship, or appropriated to it, but such as (in their common use and custom) men in those times and countries used to express their grief by it. For rending the clothes, and putting dust and ashes on the head, we have an example in Tamar's case, 2 Sam. 13:19, and for putting on sackcloth in Benhadad's servants, 1 Kings 20:31. So, we read in Joshua 7:6, that in prayer he and the Elders "fell down to the ground on their faces." So did our Savior, Matt. 26:39. But this gesture was not peculiar to God's service, but such as was taken from the civil use of those times and countries to express their reverence to their superiors, in that manner, as we see in the example of Ruth, Ruth 2:10. So their teachers were accustomed to sit, when they taught the Scribes, (Matt. 23:2). Our Savior did this as well, (Matt. 5:1 and 13:2 and 26:25; Luke 5:3 and 4:20; John 8:2). The Apostles did this, Acts 8:11, on the same ground without a doubt, because (in civil use) men were accustomed by that posture of their body to express that which they did in their places. They did this with authority and not as private men, as appears by that phrase so often used, (Psalm 69:12; Prov. 2:8; 1 Kings 29:27).

2. The second rule that concerns our reverent behavior in the whole worship of God is this. More liberty may be taken in private and secret duties of God's worship, then in public, and that both in the use of outward gestures, and in forbearing their use. 1. Knocking of the breast (as Luke 18:13) in a private prayer (though the place was public in the text) lifting up the eyes and hands to heaven, sighing and groaning, and shedding of tears, use of the voice, yes, and the extension of it by

crying and roaring, may fitly be used in secret prayer. But not so in public worship, because danger and appearance of hypocrisy may be in it if we use these before others. If we go beyond the rest of the congregation in this, our Savior (Matt. 6:16-17) charges us carefully to conceal from men all shows and appearances of our private devotion. Therefore, in Neh. 2:4, Nehemiah prayed, but used no gesture.

2. In secret prayer we may pray in our bed lying all along, and on horseback, and at our tables sitting; but in the congregation to do so could not be without evil example, and so offensive and scandalous.

3. The third rule is, outward gestures may be omitted when we cannot use them without evident danger of health, or with such pain to the body as would distract and trouble the mind in God's service. For 1. God prefers mercy before sacrifice, (Matt. 12:7). 2. No outward gesture can be acceptable to God when it hinders the service of the heart and spirit.

The *rules* that concern the whole public worship of God in general, are five. 1. The first of them is this: that for the reverence of God's public worship, care must be taken that the place where the congregation assembles may be decent and comely. It is true, it is neither needful nor fit that our temples should be either for building or furniture so glorious and rich as was that of Jerusalem. Of that it was said, Jer. 17:12, "a glorious high throne from the beginning is the place of our sanctuary." For the stateliness of that house was ceremonial and typical, it was a type of the spiritual grace and glory of the body and kingdom of Christ Jesus, as is plain by that which we read in John 1:14 and 26 compared with John 2:19, 21. It has been the folly and superstition of the Papists to think that their temples could ever be (for their building and furniture) stately and glorious enough; or that the magnificence and rich ornaments of these temples adds anything to the worship that is done to God in them. When our Savior heard some admiring the building of the temple, and how it was garnished with goodly stones and consecrated things, he reproved their folly, and said to them. "Are these the things that ye look upon," (Luke 21:5-6). 2. Neither is that holiness to be ascribed, or reverence due to our temples, as there was to that; God's special presence was tied, to that place his eye and his heart should be there continually, (2 Chron. 7:16). Of that temple the Lord said he had "hallowed it, to put his Name there forever," and a special promise was made to the prayers made in that temple, (2 Chron. 7:15). "Mine eyes shall be open and my ears attend to the prayer made in this place." Therefore, God's people esteemed that the best and fittest place even for their private and secret prayers, as we see in the examples both of Anna, (Luke 2:37), and of the good publican, (Luke 18:10). And when they could not go there to pray, yet they were accustomed to make their private prayers towards the temple, (Dan. 6:10). But we do not find that they ever showed that reverence and respect to any of their synagogues. They were not accustomed to go into their synagogues to make private prayer. Our Savior makes note that such an action had only been the fashion of *hypocrites*, (Matt. 6:5). I say that such holiness is not to be ascribed, neither is there such reverence due to our temples. They are never a bit more holy then our houses are, neither is God's presence tied to them, but to the congregation, and God's people assembled, and the exercises of religion performed in them. They are never a bit more fit as places to make our private prayers in, then our own houses and chambers are. Then, when you pray (he means this of private prayer) "enter into thy closet," our Savior says, (Matt. 6:6). 3. There is not that necessity of a temple for God's worship now, as there was for the ceremonial worship that was commanded under the Law: for that might be performed in no other place but in the temple, (Deut. 12:13-14). In so much as when the temple was profaned by idolatry and shut up from God's people as in the days of Ahaz, (2 Chron. 28:24). So, as they could not possibly come into it; and for seventy years together while they were in captivity, yet they did not dare presume, no, not in this case of necessity, to do it in any other place. But the public service of God now is not so tied to any temple, but that when we cannot have temples to do it in, it may be performed every bit as acceptably to God, and as much for the comfort of God's people, in another place. Our Savior preached sometimes in the mountains (Matt. 5:1-2). Sometimes out of a ship, (Mark 4:1-2). Sometimes in private houses, (Mark 2:2). So did Paul, (Acts 28:30-31). So, for public prayer, the godly used it sometimes in private houses, (Acts 1:13-14). Sometimes by the rivers side, (Acts 16:13). The sacrament of baptism has been administered in a private house, (Acts 10:48 and 16:33). And the sacrament of the Lord's Supper also, (Acts 20:7-8). But though all this is true, yet it is so even of our temples. Why? 1. It is fit we should have some places to assemble in, that are set apart for this purpose. And when we may have such, God's public worship is nowhere so well performed as in the temple. Therefore, Christ's custom was chiefly to preach in the synagogues and temples, (John 18:20). 2. For the reverence of God's public worship, care should be had, that the place where the congregation assembles, may be decent and comely. And that there should be some outward beauty and comeliness in those things that are used in God's service. It is noted as an argument of the holiness of the centurion, and love he bare to the Jew's religion, that he built them a synagogue, and at his charge provided them a fit place to worship God in. And our Savior when he heard it, was the rather moved to go and help his servant, (Luke 7:5-6). And our Savior (as little as he regarded stateliness and pomp in the whole course of his life) yet he made choice of an upper chamber that was large and trimmed, and prepared to celebrate the Passover, and the Lord's Supper in, (Mark 14:15).

The second general rule is, at our coming into the congregation, and during the whole time of our abode in the congregation, we should behave ourselves reverently. We may not come into this place, as we would do into a dancing school, or play-house, leaping, or laughing, or such. Neither may we go out of this place, as we would do out of such a one. But in our very coming in, and going out, and whole outward carriage we should have to give some signification of the reverence that we bear to this place, and that we do indeed account it the House of God. When God had revealed himself to Jacob in Bethel, and he perceived that God was in that place and he was not aware (and I showed you the last time, that the Lord is in a special sort present in our Church-assemblies also) it is said, he was *moved with reverence* (as the best translators read it) and said, "how reverent is this place, this is none other than the House of God, and this is the gate of heaven," (Gen. 28:6-7). So David also professes he would go to God's house *in the multitude of his mercies*, and in *his fear he would worship towards his holy Temple*, (Psalm 5:7). All things that are done in the Congregation should be done "to edifying," (1 Cor. 14:26). We should so carry ourselves, as our good example in this, so that it may edify and stir up reverence in others, and not so as we may grieve and give offence to others.

The third general rule is this. We must come all to the beginning of God's public worship, and tarry until the service is done. See this in Zech. 8:21, "And the inhabitants of one city, shall go to another, saying, let us go speedily to pray before the Lord, and to seek the Lord of Hosts, I will go also." Ezek. 46:10, "The Prince shall go in, when they go in, and when they go forth, they shall go forth together." Yes, it is the duty of God's people in reverence of his public worship, to be here before the beginning. It becomes them to wait for the minister of God, and *not to let him wait for them*. The conversion of the Gentiles is noted by this sign that (they shall so love the word of Christ that) "they shall wait for his Law," (Isaiah 42:4). And to such hearers is the blessing promised, Proverbs 8:34, "Blessed is the man that heareth me, watching daily at my gates, and giving attendance at the posts of my doors." It is said of Cornelius (and yet he was a great man and a captain) that when he had sent for Peter, he called together his kinsfolk, and special friends, before Peter came, and waited for him, (Acts 10:24). And the people should also be tarrying until the end. We have a notable example in Luke 1:21. Though the public worship that Zachariah the priest performed were not

40

such as the people could make use of, as our people may make of everything that the minister uses in our assemblies, and though Zachariah tarried much longer than ordinary, yet they waited until *he* had finished, and would not go away until he had dismissed them, and given them the blessing.

The reasons of this are two. 1. There is nothing done in our assemblies, but all may receive profit by it. 1. By the confession of sin and all other prayers used in the congregation, a man may receive more profit and comfort then by any other. That is the reason why the Apostles (even after the ascension of Christ, when the typical honor of the temple was abolished, and it had no more holiness in it then our temples have) were so delighted to go to the temple to pray, at the times of public prayer, (Acts 3:1 and 22:17). And all the godly women at Philippi even with peril of their lives, were accustomed every Sabbath to meet together, only for prayer, (Acts 16:13). 2. By hearing of the word read in the congregation, all may profit, as you may see in Deut. 31:12-13, "Thou shalt read this law, before all Israel in their hearing that they may hear and that they may learn to fear the Lord your God and observe to do all the words of this law." 3. By hearing the word preached, even by the meanest minister of Christ, all may profit, if the fault is not in themselves, (James 1:21). It is able to save our souls, (1 Cor. 14:21). "Ye may all prophecy one by one," that all may learn, and may have comfort. 4. The singing of psalms in the congregation furthers the fruit of the word in the hearts of all the hearers. When the Apostle exhorts the faithful that they would let the word of Christ dwell in them richly in all wisdom, (Col. 3:16), he tells them that (to that end) they should "teach and admonish one another in psalms and hymns and spiritual songs." 5. All the faithful may receive benefit by the sacrament of the Lord's Supper, (1 Cor. 10:16). "The cup of blessing which we bless, is it not the communion of the blood of Christ? The bread which we break, is it not the communion of the body of Christ?" 6. By being present at the administration of baptism, all may receive profit, for by it we are put in mind of the covenant that God made with us in our baptism, and the benefit that was sealed to us by it. That which is said by the Apostle in Romans 4:11 of circumcision, may be said likewise of baptism that is *come into the room of it, it is a seal of the righteousness which is by faith.* And we are also by this reminded of the covenant we made with God in our baptism, of which it is good we are often put in mind, as appears by the care Joshua had to set up a great stone by the sanctuary to keep in the remembrance of the people, the covenant they had made with God, (Joshua 24:26-27). Thereby, also we perform a duty of love to the infant and his parents, and to do good (in this kind especially) we should not forget, for with such sacrifices (and fruits of our love) God is well pleased, (Heb. 13:16). 7. By the blessing pronounced by God's minister, all may receive good. When Aaron and his sons should bless the people, the Lord says they should "put his name upon the children of Israel, and he would bless them," (Num. 6:27). When the Priest and the Levites blessed the people, (2 Chron. 30:27), it is said, "Their cry was heard, and their prayer came up to heaven, his holy habitation."

2. Though we could receive no profit by the exercises used in our assemblies, yet we must be present at them all, to do our homage to God, and show the reverent respect we have to his ordinances. For there is nothing to be done in God's public worship among us, but it is to be done by the institution and ordinance and commandment of the Lord.

1. It is his ordinance that whenever the congregation assembles, there should be all sorts and kinds of prayer used. Yes, this is a chief duty to be performed in our assemblies, 1. Tim. 2:1-2, "I exhort therefore, that first of all supplications, prayers, intercessions, and giving of thanks be made for all men. For Kings and for all that are in authority," *etc.*

2. It is his ordinance that in our public assemblies the word of God should be read, Deut. 31:11-12, "When all Israel is come to appear before the Lord thy God in the place which he shall choose, thou shalt read this law before all Israel in their hearing: Gather the people together, men, women and children, and thy stranger that is within thy gates, that they may hear, and that they may learn and fear the Lord your God, and observe to do all the words of this law." And it is plain by Acts 13:15, compared with Acts 15:21, that it was the custom of the Jews (while they continued to be the true Church and people of God) to read the Law and the Prophets (the whole Canonical Scripture) in all their Synagogues every Sabbath day.

3. It is his ordinance that the word should be preached, interpreted, and applied in our public assemblies. Eccl. 4:17, "When you go into the house of God be more ready to hear," *etc.* Acts 15:21, "Moses after he

was read, was preached in the Synagogue every Sabbath day."

4. It is his ordinance that the Lord's Supper should be administered in the public assemblies. It was not only the custom of the people of God in Corinth to receive this sacrament in the Church and place of their public assemblies as is plain by that which the Apostle writes, 1 Cor. 11:22, but they are also charged and commanded by him to do so in verses 33-34, "Wherefore my brethren, when ye come together to eat (*the Lord's Supper he means, as appears plainly by that which went before*) tarry one for another; And if any man hunger, let him eat at home, that ye come not together unto condemnation."

5. It is his ordinance that Baptism should be administered in the public assemblies; as John administered it in a solemn assembly, so our Savior when he desired it, did not send for John to come to him to Nazareth to administer it, but came (though a long journey, fourteen miles as Geographers think) from Nazareth to Bethabara, where John used to baptize, Matt. 3:13.

6. It is God's ordinance that in our public assemblies psalms should be sung, for as it is evident by their titles that they were penned for the use of the whole church in the most solemn worship of God; so were they used accordingly not only by David, 1 Chron. 16:4-7, and Jehoshaphat, 2 Chron. 20:21-22, and Jehu did, 2 Chron. 33:15, and Hezekiah, 2 Chron. 29:30, but by our blessed Savior himself also did this at the celebration of the Passover and of his holy Supper, Matt. 26:38. Yes, it is plain by Psalm 81:4,[16] that there was a direct

commandment and law of God that required them so to do.

7. It is his ordinance that the minister should dismiss the congregation, by pronouncing God's blessing on them, Num. 6:23, Deut. 10:8 and 21:5, so that to refuse to come to any part of God's public worship, or to go away before all is done, is a disgrace and contempt done to the ordinance of God.

The fourth general rule is this, we must (when we are present) join with the congregation in all the parts of God's worship, and do as the congregation does. I do not speak of every congregation, but of a congregation of the faithful, of a congregation that is instructed and reformed according to the word of God. It makes much for the comeliness and reverence of God's worship, that all things in the congregation be done in good order, and without confusion, 1 Cor. 14:40. Paul being absent from them, rejoiced to think on the reverent and good order that was in the assemblies of the Colossians, (Col. 2:5). And it is a principal part of the good order that should be in the congregation when they all come together, and go together, pray together, sing together, and kneel together. In a word, when every part of God's worship is so performed by the congregation they should consider it as if the whole congregation were but one man. If it is otherwise, there is a great confusion, when while some are hearing, others are praying; some sing, and some are silent. Therefore, it is said, Neh. 8:1, "All the people assembled themselves as one man," and Acts 2. 46. "They continued daily in the temple, with joint consent," as if

---

[16] "For this was a statute for Israel, and a law of the God of Jacob," (Psalm 81:4).

they all had but one heart. And it is not fit for any Christian, either to come short of, or go beyond the congregation in gestures of reverence and devotion in the public worship of God.

The fifth and last general rule is this, we must teach our servants and children to show reverence to the sanctuary and public worship of God. Men may not suffer their children and servants to show contempt to it. The keeping of the Sabbath, and reverence of the sanctuary are coupled together twice in Lev. 19:30 and 26:2, because no man can keep the Sabbath well, that does not give reverence to the sanctuary. And for the Sabbath, you know, God does not credit us with observing it unless we see to it that our children and servants observe it also, Exod. 20:11. No man should say If I myself reverence God's sanctuary, it does not matter if I have in my house those who despise it. Abraham had been never better, nor more assured of God's blessing for serving God himself, if he had not commanded his sons and his household after him to do so too, Gen. 18:19. David vowed to God that no deceitful person (that had a hollow heart towards religion) should dwell in his house, Psalm 101:7. Did he dare, you think, to have kept anyone that was an open despiser of Religion? Neither let any say, this does not apply to children and it doesn't matter what behavior they use in church, even if they prate or play, or cry in disturbing the congregation. For I tell you, God cannot endure profaneness or contempt of religion, no not in children, as is plain by his fearful judgment on the children of Bethel, for scorning his prophet in 2 Kings 2:23-24. Yes, it stands on all of us to use the uttermost authority we have to maintain the reverence of God's sanctuary. For, the open contempt done by any, may bring God's curse on us all. Did not Achan the Son of Zerah commit a trespass in the accursed thing, (Phineas says in Joshua 22:20), and wrath fell on the entire congregation of Israel? And that man did not perish alone in his iniquity. And certainly, among other causes of the plague and other judgments of God on the land, this is not the least, that God's public worship is performed among us with so little reverence and devotion as it is. For this cause (the Apostle says, 1 Cor. 11:30) many are weak and sickly among you, and many sleep (*i.e.* have died).

CHAPTER 3:
TRUE RELIGION

We come now to the question itself, which this woman at the well propounds to our Savior, in which (that we may the better receive our instruction from it) these three things are to be observed.

1. That (perceiving him to be a Prophet, and one that could tell secrets) she sought not to know her fortune (as we say) how long she should live, how many more husbands she should have, or how many children, what manner of ones they would prove, or such matters. If she would have yielded to that curiosity, that is in us all by nature, she would have questioned him about such things. But, being effectually touched in her conscience by the Spirit of God with remorse for her sin, and desire of salvation, she only seeks to be instructed by him in a chief ground of religion, and case of conscience.

2. Though this woman was a Samaritan, and a harlot, yet she took notice of a main controversy that was between the Jews and Samaritans about the right way to salvation, and true manner of serving God. Yes, she was acquainted also with the chief reason that the Samaritans alleged for themselves.

3. She does not satisfy her conscience in the long custom of all her neighbors and antiquity of their religion. She also does not fear the imputation of lightness and inconstancy among her neighbors. Rather, she calls into question the religion which herself and all her ancestors had professed, and earnestly desires to be resolved by Christ, whether it is the true religion or not. And from

this example in this way considered, we have this *doctrine* to learn for our instruction: that every Christian, even such women, are bound to seek to be resolved, and settled in the knowledge of the true religion of God. Before I come to prove this, two things are to be premised to rightly understand the doctrine.

1. I do not say that everyone is bound to study controversies, so as to be able to answer an adversary. For this is a special gift required of the minister to be able to convince the adversary, (Titus. 1:9), and to stop his mouth, (verse 11). Yes, it may do hurt to a weak Christian, to busy himself much with controversies, to read the books written by adversaries to the truth, or confer with them, (Romans 14:1). Those that are weak in the faith, receive them, but not for controversies in disputing.

2. I do not say that there is the same measure of knowledge required of every Christian. For 1. Of us that live in these days (in which the light is so clearly revealed, in which, besides the ministry of the word, there are books of all sorts written) more knowledge is required, than was of our forefathers. 2. Of such as live under the better means of instruction, more is required, then those that live under a dumb and ignorant ministry. The apostle sharply reproves the Hebrews in 5:12 for that (whereas, considering the time they lived in, and means they had enjoyed, they ought to have been teachers, yet had need to be taught their first principles. He tells them, Heb. 6:1, 3, that unless they were careful to grow forward to perfection, they were in great danger to fall into the unpardonable sin. 3. Of such as have more leisure, and fewer distractions through worldly business, God requires a greater measure of knowledge then of others.

That which the Apostle speaks of unmarried people holds good proportion with gentlemen and others, that (by reason of their estates) they are freed from that toil in worldly business that others have, (1 Cor. 7:32). The unmarried care for the things of the Lord, "how he may please the Lord," (verse 33). He that is married cares for the things of the world. 4. Of such as God has given best natural parts, best minds, and best memories to, he requires more knowledge then of others. For Christ says in general, "To whomsoever much is given, of him shall be much required," (Luke 12:48).

The doctrine remains true, that every Christian (of whatever sex and condition they are) is bound to seek to be resolved and settled in the knowledge of the true religion of God. Observe the confirmation of this doctrine in three points.

1. Everyone is bound to seek the knowledge of the truth. 1 Tim. 2:4, "God would have all men (all sorts) to be saved;" but how? "to come to the knowledge of the truth." Though the Lord is infinite in mercy, yet they can have no comfort in his mercy, that have no knowledge in it. Isaiah 27:11, "It is a people of no understanding, therefore he that hath made them, shall have no compassion of them, and he that formed them, shall have no mercy on them." Say a man leads an honest and virtuous life, that will not serve his turn, without knowledge. 2 Peter 1:5, "Join to your virtue knowledge." Say a man has a good meaning, and is devout and careful to please God; this will do him no good without knowledge. Romans 10:2, the Jews had the "zeal of God, but it was not according to knowledge;" and therefore for

all their zeal the "wrath of God came on them to the utmost," (1 Thess. 2:16).

2. No man is to content himself with some smattering, or small measure of knowledge, but everyone is bound to seek for certain truth, and to have a sound judgement, and settled resolution in the matters of his religion, Romans 14:5. Let every man be fully persuaded in his mind, that he may be able to say, as, Romans 14:14, "I know and am persuaded through the Lord Jesus." And Paul's prayer to God for the Colossians was (and if he desired it for them, they were bound to desire it for themselves) that they might know the mysteries of religion in all riches of the full assurance of understanding. Col. 2:2 and verse 7 requires, that they would seek to be "rooted, and established in the faith." And Peter reports of all the faithful he wrote to, that they had knowledge and were "stablished" in the present truth. 2 Peter 1:12. And 2 Peter 3:17, "Beware least ye fall from your own steadfastness;" verse 18, "but grow in grace and in the knowledge of our Lord." And Paul tells the Colossians in chapter 1:22-23, that Christ will present them "holy and unblameable unto God, if they continue in the faith, grounded and settled and be not moved away from the hope of the Gospel." Though it is not required of every Christian to be able to answer everything that is objected, yet should he be, *propositi tenax*, "so sure of that truth," which he has learned from God's word, that nothing that is objected by any adversary, may draw him from it. 1 Cor. 2:15, "He that is spiritual discerneth all things, and he is judged of no man." Insomuch, as though the learned man in the world, yes an angel from heaven, should object against it, yet he would not yield to him,

(Gal. 1:8-9). In this respect the faithful man is compared to a tree that grows by the rivers of water, and is well rooted. But the hypocrite to the chaff, (Psalm 1:3-4).

3. Everyone that has means is bound so far forth to take notice of the controversies of religion, as may serve for settling his own heart in the truth. 1 Cor. 14:20, "Brethren, be not children in understanding, but of a ripe age." Phil. 1:9-10, "And this, I pray, that your love may abound yet more and more in knowledge, and in all judgement," and verse 11, "that you may allow those things that are best that you may be pure and without offence until the day of Christ." It is the commandment of God to his people, Jer. 6:16, that they would stand in the ways, and "behold, and ask for the old way, which is the good way." When a man sees there are diverse ways, and broad ones too, it is not good to go on carelessly, but he should stand still, and consider, and behold, which is the better and more likely way, and ask of such as can direct him. It would be a good confirmation to a Christian (that has means to direct him) to compare the doctrine of Papists with ours, and the weak grounds they have to build on.

1. Our religion is our chief inheritance, Psalm 119:111, "and our glory" Psalm 4:2. Every one seeks certainty in his inheritance. If he sees any holes in his lease, or evidence, he will give no rest to himself, nor spare cost, until he has made it sure.

2. It is necessary to the salvation of every man, that he professes the true religion, and be a member of the true church. For out of the true church and religion, no man can find assurance of salvation and comfort. See the necessity of this profession in Romans 10:10, "With the

mouth man confesseth to salvation." Isaiah 44:5, "One shall say, I am the Lord's, another shall be called by the name of Jacob: another shall subscribe with his hand to the Lord, and surname himself by the name of Israel." Mark how the profession of the true religion, yes, the very hope of salvation, and joining to the true church, goes together. So, Noah desiring the salvation of Japheth's posterity prays that God would persuade Japheth to dwell in the tents of Shem, (Gen. 9:27). And 2 Chron. 11:16, "All such as set their hearts to seek God, came to Jerusalem." So it is said, "God added to the Church such as should be saved," (Acts 2:47). And it was David's comfort and glory, that he was the son of God's handmaid, (Psalm 116:16), as if he should not else have been God's servant. Therefore, the true religion and church is called often *the Kingdom of heaven,* (Matt. 13:44, 47). And that promise that is made, Isaiah 33:24, (the people that dwell there shall have their sins forgiven) though it is to be understood of the universal church, as it is in our creed, and not of any particular visible church, yet may it in this way be applied to the church which is visible, as that a man may say boldly, "none can ordinarily attain to salvation, that is not a member of the true visible church." Now there is but one true church and religion. There may be in matters of less moment, various differences in the true church (as between us and the Lutherans, and Brownists, and among ourselves) but these do not make us several churches. In the fundamental points of religion, (the knowledge of which is absolutely necessary to salvation, and the profession of this makes a true Christian) we all agree. It is a damnable conceit of some, that a man may be saved in any religion.

There is but one faith, (Eph. 4:5), one way to life, and one gate, (Matt. 7:13). God's promise is to all his elect, that he will give them one heart, and one way, (Jer. 32:39). It stands to men, therefore, to enquire diligently which is the only true church, which is the only true religion.

3. Such as are not well grounded in religion, and careful to attain a certainty and resolution in it, are in a continual danger to be seduced, and to fall from their profession, either on the right hand or on the left. The Apostle gives the reason why he desired the Colossians might attain to all riches of the full assurance of understanding lest any should beguile them, (Col. 2:24). That is by way of *halting*, for they are easily turned out of the way, and therefore it is necessary to go steadily and strongly in the right way, (Heb. 12:13). They that are children in understanding and wavering, will be easily carried away with every wind of vain doctrine, (Eph. 4:14). Whom did the seducers in old times prevail with? 2 Tim. 3:6-7, with simple women that were ever learning, and never able to come to the knowledge of the truth. And 2 Peter 2:14, with unstable souls. And do not wonder at this, for (though we are accustomed to wonder at the absurdities of every contrary religion; and think a simple man may easily be able to answer, whatever they can say; and the confidence we have in ourselves this way, is a chief cause why we do not more carefully seek to ground ourselves in the knowledge of the truth) yet, it is certain, that the grossest adversaries of the truth are able to use such reasons and persuasions as have in them a great probability and show of truth. The Apostle says of the seducers of his time, that they had, Col. 2:4, παραλογίζηται ἐν πιθανολογίᾳ, and Eph. 4:14, τῇ κυβείᾳ

τῶν ἀνθρώπων, a notable vein in persuading; a great deal of cunning, even such as cheaters at dice use with a great amount of craft to beguile and circumvent them that they deal with.

4. No man can be saved, unless he is willing to suffer for his religion, yes, even to die for it, "If any man will come after me," our Savior says, Luke 9:23, "let him deny himself and take up his cross daily and follow me." And Luke 14:26, "If any man come to me and hate not his own life, that is, be not willing to part with it for my sake, he cannot be my disciple." And Rev. 3:10, "Be thou faithful unto death and I will give thee the crown of life." And who can do that but he that is well grounded and certain of the truth of his religion? No man can have peace in his conscience, nor comfort in the evil day, in the hour of death or time of great affliction, that is uncertain in his religion.

5. A good conscience that gives a man assurance that he is in the state of grace, in the right way to life, will yield a man unspeakable comfort at all times. When a man is sure that God accepts his work, then may he well say to himself, "Go eat thy bread with joy, and drink thy wine with a cheerful heart," (Eccl. 9:7). Yes, in the time of greatest affliction, such a one may have much comfort. On the other hand, how can he have comfort in that day when he is unresolved? When he shall consider that he must either go to heaven or hell, and that there is but one way to heaven? Whether he is uncertain if he is in that one way or not? How can he choose but to be in extreme perplexity? As the man that travels in a tempestuous weather, ready to be benighted, and does not know the way, and is sure that if he misses the right way, he shall

fall into the hands of thieves, or other certain perils of his life. He must necessarily be in extreme fear and anguish of heart. It is this way in this case. Such a man like this prays regularly, and does good works, yet, all this can yield him no comfort if he is without Christ or the truth. He that doubts (the Apostle says in Romans 14:23) is "condemned if he eat, because he doth it not of faith." And, "whatever is not of faith, is sin." Even the doubts that the faithful feel in themselves (though they are not quite void of faith and certainty) cause much discomfort to them as it appears by the tears that that poor man shed by his unbelief, (Mark 9:24), and by that sadness and sorrow of heart, which the two disciples of Emmaus felt in themselves when they doubted whether Christ was the true Messiah, (Luke 24:17). How much more will people like this have no faith, no certainty at all mixed with them? Therefore, the Lord bids them that would find rest to their souls, use all the means to find out the good way and walk in it, (Jer. 6:16). And the Apostle gives this for a reason, that he so much desired that the Colossians might attain to all riches of the assurance of understanding, that their "hearts might be comforted," (Col. 2:2).

2. The example of the Papists. Though this has been a main principal in their religion, that ignorance is the mother of devotion, yet now even women among them grow perfect and ready in the grounds of their religion, and are able to give a reason of that they hold, and to teach their children also. And what shame is that for us?

1. For exhortation to diligence in the use of all means whereby we may grow to certainty in our religion. 1. We must live under and frequent an ordinary ministry.

For that is ordained for this end, that we may be no longer as children tossed to and fro with every wind of doctrine, (Eph. 4:14). And ye hear of few seduced either by Papists or Brownists, that enjoyed an ordinary and settled ministry. 2. We must give ourselves to reading of good books, specially of the Scriptures; for they are able to make us wise to salvation, (2 Timothy 3:15). 3. We must use our doubts to confer and move questions to such as are able to help us, "the priests lips should keep knowledge, so the people should seek the law at his mouth," (Malachi 2:7). And Cornelius was directed to send for Peter and to seek resolution in all his doubts from him, (Acts 10:5, 32). 4. Because only the Lord is the teacher that can resolve and persuade our hearts. We must give ourselves much to humble and faithful prayer, as David did, Psalm 119:18, "Open thou mine eyes," *etc.* So did the spouse of Christ, when she found herself in danger to be seduced, (Song of Songs 1:7), and Cornelius being in doubt and perplexity this day, sought by fasting and prayer to receive direction and resolution from God, (Acts 10:30).

2. For reproof, 1. Of those that willingly remain unsettled in religion upon this pretense, that by reason of the many differences in religion they find in the world, and the great show of reason each side has, and the foul faults that they discern in men of all religions, they see great cause to doubt them all, and have a small hope to attain to any certainty. Therefore, they will serve God, and not trouble themselves to enquire which side has the truth. For the elect, and such as have grace, and good hearts, shall be able to attain to certainty, though there are never so many great differences and occasions of

doubting. Of the elect it is said, Matt. 24:24, that it is not possible for them to be deceived, and John 10:4-5, that Christ's sheep "know" his voice and "will follow" him; and a stranger "they will not follow," because they do not know his voice. And of the godly and such as use the means of grace and knowledge with a good heart, it is said, that the "Light shall shine upon their ways," (Job 22:28). That God will instruct and teach them in the way that they should go and guide them with his eye, (Psalm 32:8). That the "secret of the Lord" is revealed to them that fear him; and his covenant to give them understanding, (Psalm 25:14). That their ears shall hear a word behind them, saying, "this is the way walk ye in it," (Isaiah 30:21). That they shall know of that doctrine which is taught them, whether it is of God, or whether their teacher speaks of himself, (John 7:17). That they have an unction from the holy one, and know all things, (John 2:20). Such shall understand the Scripture and grow to certainty. For the testimony of the Lord is sure, "and maketh wise the simple," (Psalm 19:7). It is able to give subtilty to the simple, and to the child knowledge and discretion, (Prov. 1:4). So that all such as resolve that they will remain in the middle, and do not seek certainty, these give evidence against themselves, that they do not belong to God's election, nor have any grace in them.

2. Those that are ignorant and utterly unacquainted with matters of religion, that think and speak of these things carelessly, or as of things that do not concern them. Such are the most, even of those that have best leisure, and best minds and memories, to Hosea 8:12 may be applied, "I have written to them the great things of my Law, but they are counted as a strange thing." But

how well such people judge themselves, the Holy Ghost pronounces them to be plain atheists and condemners of God, as you shall see, Job 21:14-15, they (do in deed and heart) say "unto God depart from us, that say we desire not the knowledge of thy ways," yes, such say in their hearts, "what is the Almighty that we should serve him, and what profit should we have if we pray unto him."

3. Such as (though they approve of the truth) wish well to them that profess it, (and profess it themselves) yet they do this on no other grounds then that the state, and place we live in, *those people* profess it, or that such and such good men teach and hold to it. Where, we should not receive our religion on any man's credit, but labor to see its grounds with our own eyes. The people of God are not drawn to a resolution in religion by company or compulsion, but on their free choice. They examine it, (Matt. 13:44; Acts 17:11), and see good reason and ground for it. On this they advisedly and voluntarily choose it, Psalm 119:30, "I have chosen the way of truth: and thy judgements have I laid before me." So as they are able to say, "We believe and know," (John 6:69). We should be able to give a reason why we hold religion in the way we do, (1 Peter 3:15). And it is noted for the property of the unsound hearted hearer, Mark 4:6, "That he receiveth with gladness immediately what he hears," without ever examining it before. The faith and religion most men have, is rather sucked in with their mother's milk, then received by the instruction of their teachers. They hold it, because it is commonly believed, not because it is certainly true. It is not chosen by them on their own judgement, but taken in on common credit.

CHAPTER 4:
TRADITION

We have considered what the question was that troubled the mind of this woman, and in which she desired to be resolved by our Savior; namely, concerning the true church and religion of God, which is the second part of this text. It follows now, its third and last part. Namely, the reason that moved her to doubt this matter, and to be perplexed in her mind about this question. It was this: on the one side her fathers had worshipped God in Mount Gerizim, and that made her think that place was the best place to serve God in; and on the other side, Christ, whom she knew to be a prophet, and all others that were of his religion, said, that Jerusalem was the place where men ought to worship. So, that made her doubt that she had served God amiss all this while. In this, we have to observe, that the Samaritans made the example and custom and authority of their forefathers the rule and warrant of their religion, and that was the point which deceived them.

And from there we learn this doctrine: that it is not safe but dangerous in matters of religion to ascribe too much to antiquity, and to the example and custom of our forefathers. But before I confirm this doctrine, lest any should think we make no account of antiquity, or of the example and authority of our forefathers, four things shall be premised for the right understanding of this doctrine, concerning the account that is to be made in matters of religion, 1. Of antiquity. 2. Of our forefathers. 3.

Of our natural parents and ancestors. 4. Of the customs of the places in which we live.

1. There is an antiquity which is a certain and infallible note of the true religion. The old way is called "the good way," (Jer. 6:16). The true Religion is the most ancient religion. So, the prophets that seduced God's people to idolatry are said to have caused them to stumble in their way from the ancient ways, (Jer. 18:15). So, the idolatry of the Jews is disgraced by this note that it was new, (Deut. 32:17). They served new gods newly come up. And the true church of God is called, "The ancient people," (Isaiah 44:7). No people of any religion in the world may compare in antiquity with the true church of God. But that is only truly ancient in matters of religion, which was from the beginning.

It is not the continuance of a thousand or two thousand years that can make anything in religion truly ancient; but it must be from the beginning, or it is not truly ancient. The Gospel is called an eternal Gospel, (Rev. 14:6). And so John commends his doctrine, 1 John 1:1, to be that which "was from the beginning." So, our Savior gives this rule to try truth in religion by, Matt. 19:8, "From the beginning it was not so." And the Apostle, 1 Cor. 11:23, grounds his doctrine of the sacrament, and the direction he gives to the church about it, on its first institution. That is truly ancient in matters of religion that can fetch his origin from him that is called the Ancient of Days, (Dan. 7:9), that is, from God himself and his word. That such things derived from men is not ancient in this case. So, the Lord in that place I cited even now, (Deut. 32:17), calls the idolatry of the Israelites "the worshipping of new gods newly come up" (though they had continued in the world many hundred years. For Abraham's ancestors were idolaters, Joshua 24:2, because it was but the device of man, and had no warrant from his word. That which is grounded on the authority of the prophets and apostles, which wrote by divine inspiration, that, and that alone, has true antiquity for it. This made John say, 1 John 2:7, "the old commandment" is the word. So that whatever doctrine is taught and confirmed by the authority of the word, though it may seem new to men, because they never heard of it before, yet it is *not new* in itself. Neither can they that teach or receive it, be justly called novelists or new-fangled men. It was not an innovation or new-fangledness in Nehemiah to celebrate the feast of the Tabernacles, (Nehemiah 8:17), though it had been out of use from the days of Joshua to that time. This was because it had the warrant and authority of the word of God. And whatever doctrine is taught, or custom received in the church, without the warrant and authority of the word, though it could be proved to have been taught and received one thousand six hundred years ago, by such and such famous men, and ancient churches, yet it is a novelty, and has no true antiquity to commend it to us.

2. As we have this to say for antiquity, so we also of our forefathers, that there are certain fathers whose example ought to be of great authority with us in matters of religion. "Remember the days of old (saith the Lord)," (Deut. 32:7). "Consider the years of so many generations; ask thy father, and he will show thee, thine elders and they will tell thee." And Job 8:8, "Inquire of the former age, and prepare thyself to search of their fathers." And it is often noted, as Deut. 32:17 and Jer. 44:3, to aggravate

the sin of the Jews that they served new gods, newly come up, gods whom their "fathers knew not." So that if we should walk in a new way that our elders and forefathers had not walked in, we have a just cause to fear we are not in the right way. Our Savior directing his church how to find the right way, bids her to observe the steps of the old flock," (Song 1:8 and Jer. 18:15). He calls "the false way," a way that was "not trodden." But these fathers that should be of such authority with us in matters of religion, are to have followed the direction of the word. Amon is blamed for forsaking the God of his fathers (2 Kings 21:22). Yet he walked in the way of his own father, and of most of his ancestors; yes, it is expressly said, that he "did evil in the sight of the Lord, as his father Manasseh did," (verse 20). How is it then said, that he forsook the God of his fathers? The reason is rendered in the same place, in verse 22, "because he walked not in the way of the Lord." Those are the fathers we are to have respect to in the matters of religion, that walk *in the way of the Lord*, and *none but they*. So that, as our Savior says, Matt. 12:50, "Whosoever shall do my Father's will which is in heaven, he is my brother, and sister, and mother." So, we may truly say, that all the godly that in former ages have walked in the way of the Lord, they are our fathers. And though that we did not know any of our own ancestors that professed the religion that we do, yet so long as we profess no other religion then the patriarchs, prophets and apostles did, and many other holy men that have lived since the apostles times, we cannot justly be said to have forsaken the God of our fathers, or to be of any other religion then our forefathers were of.

3. In some cases there is also a great respect to be had to the example even of our natural parents. It should be a great bond for a Christian to keep him in the love of the truth, when his own parents and ancestors have been lovers and professors of the true religion. This is noted to the praise of Azaria and Jotham, (2 Kings 15:3 and 34). "They did uprightly in the sight of the Lord, according to all that their fathers did." That is the reason why Paul puts Timothy in mind of the piety that was both in his mother and grandmother, (2 Tim. 1:5). And a double condemnation shall without a doubt fall on such as have had religious parents if they themselves become either papists or profane men. This is noted to the shame of the Israelites in Judges 2:17, that they "turned quickly out of the way wherein their fathers walked," obeying the commandments of God, but they did not so. And Jehoram the King of Judah received a writing from Elijah the Prophet, threatening extreme vengeance against him because he had not walked in the ways of Jehoshaphat and Asa, having so good a father, and so good a grandfather, that he yet became himself so ungracious a man, (2 Chron. 21:12-14).

4. Some authority and religious respect is also sometimes to be given even to the customs, and fashions of the places where we live. Paul alleges the custom of the churches to stop the mouth of contentious men, (1 Cor. 11:16). Good customs taken up on good grounds, received and long continued among God's people, should not lightly be broken and laid down. For the Israelites, 2 Kings 17:34, are blamed for "breaking" their customs. The Apostle commends various truths to the people of God by this argument, that they had received them and makes

that a further bond to their conscience, (1 Cor. 15:1). "I declare to you the Gospel which I preached to you, which ye also received and wherein ye continue." And Phil. 4:9, "Those things which ye have both learned and received, those things do, and the God of peace shall be with you." Yes, it is not a small sin for any private man to break the good orders and customs of the church of God, or to seek to be privileged and exempted from them. There is a general rule given to us, Prov. 2:20, "Walk in the ways of good men, and keep the ways of the righteous." God has made a promise to those that will learn the ways of his people, and conform themselves to them, (Jer. 12:16). Some say there is no law to bind us to give every Sabbath something at church to relieve the poor. Yet, the very custom of a congregation should be in accordance to the word, for the Apostle says he set this order in all the churches of Galatia, (1 Cor. 16:1). This should bind us to continue in it, and cannot be despised by any without sin. Say there were no law to bind such as have committed fornication, with the public scandal of the congregation, to profess their repentance publicly, for the satisfaction of the congregation; yet, the very custom of the congregation grounded on God's word, as this is (for the Apostle required that the fornicator should be put from among them, that is, separated from the privileges of the Church, till he had professed his repentance, (1 Cor. 5:2). And our Savior enjoins him that had given offence, but to one member of the Church, not to presume to offer his gift to God, until he had made satisfaction to his neighbor, (Matt. 5:24). And how much more respect is to be had to a whole congregation, then to any one member?) I say this very custom of the congregation in this way grounded on the word, should not be violated in favor of any man.

These four points being in this way premised, it remains that I confirm the *doctrine, viz.,* that it is dangerous in matters of religion to ascribe too much to antiquity or to the custom or example of our forefathers. For proof of this doctrine look into the holy Scriptures, and into the examples of all ages, and you shall find that the chief thing that hardens men in superstition has been the ancient custom and use of their forefathers. The prophet speaks of the Jews in his time, Jer. 9:14, "They walked after the stubbornness of their own hearts and after Balaam's which their fathers taught them." And the Apostle Peter says of them he wrote to, 1 Peter 1:18, that all their "vain conversation" was received by "tradition of their fathers." And in this place in John 4, the thing that hardened the Samaritans in their superstition, was this: their fathers worshipped in this mountain.

The reasons why it is not safe, but dangerous in matters of religion, to rely too much on antiquity and on the custom of our forefathers, are the following points.

1. Because it is evident that many of the grossest errors that ever were in religion are of great antiquity. The idolatry of the Pagans was of great antiquity. Joshua 14:2, the superstition of the Jews that hold the observation of Moses' ceremonies necessary to salvation, is of great antiquity. For it began in the apostle's days. "And certain men which came down from Judaea taught the brethren, and said, Except ye be circumcised after the manner of Moses, ye cannot be saved," (Acts 15:1). The corruptions of religion that the Pharisees held in Christ's time, were very ancient, (Matt. 5:21, 27, 33), "Ye have

heard it hath been said to them of old time," *etc.* And so, the errors of the Papists may not be denied to be very ancient. For the mystery of iniquity began to work even in the Apostles time, (2 Thess. 2:7).

2. It is no undutifulness in a child, to swerve from his father's example in anything, in which his father has swerved from the word of God. Our parents must be obeyed in the Lord, (Eph. 6:1), and are called the parents of our bodies; and the Lord the Father of our spirits and consciences, (Heb. 12:9). And in this case we have a rule, Matt. 23:9, "Call no man father upon earth, for one is your father which is in heaven."

The *use* of this doctrine is manifold. First, for justifying our religion against one of the chief objections the Papists make against it, (namely, that it is new, and no older then Luther) and for confirming our hearts against it. If this should be true, it would indeed be sufficient to prove it a false religion. But first it should not seem strange to us to have the true religion of God charged with novelty. This is an old slander, "What new doctrine is this," say the Jews of Christ's own doctrine, (Mark 1:27). "May we know what this new doctrine is whereof thou speakest," the Athenians said to Paul, (Acts 17:29). 2. It is evident by authentic stories, that this truth that we profess has had many witnesses in every age since the apostle's times, even in the darkest times of Popery. And Master Luther was God's blessed instrument to bring it to light in this last age, as Hilkiah was of finding the book of God's Law, (2 Kings 22:8). Yet, Luther was its author, no more then Hilkiah was of that. 3. Say that we could not show any that had professed it for 1500, years before Luther, yet because we hold nothing but that which has witness of the law, of the prophets, as Romans 3:21, our religion must necessarily be held to be truly ancient.

2. For defending of ourselves against the imputation of undutifulness towards our ancestors which the Papists also cast on us, as if by professing this religion we condemned all our forefathers. For first, many that lived in the midst of the darkness of Popery, were extraordinarily preserved from the gross errors of the Papists (as the three children were in the fiery furnace, Dan. 3:27) and enlightened with the knowledge of the truth, which we ourselves do now profess, as may evidently prove. Neither should this seem strange, since we know the Lord has been accustomed at such times, and in such places as he has denied the ordinary means of grace to preserve, instruct, and save his elect extraordinarily. So, he had 7000 in the ten tribes that had not once bowed their knee to Baal, (1 Kings 19:18). So, he worked faith in Rahab while she lived among the cursed Canaanites, (Heb. 11:31). And in the wise men while they lived in the East in the midst of pagans and idolaters, (Matt. 2:1-2). 2. Many that professed popery in their lifetime, might yet find mercy with him (especially in the most fundamental point of faith the doctrine of justification) at the hour of death; which we have no cause to doubt of, not only because the Scripture has revealed that the Lord uses to call some at the last hour, (Matt. 20:6-7). We find by experience, that even now-a-days, men are now far more obstinate, and more settled in popery, then our forefathers could be (as having stronger means to corrupt and poison them then they had). Though their sin is far greater than the sin of our

forefathers was because they sin against the light that is so clearly revealed. Yes, many of them have fallen into apostasy from the truth which they had formerly professed. Yet, even now-a-days many Papists find that mercy with God as to renounce popery at the hour of their death in that main doctrine of justification by works. 3. We have, rather, cause to hope and judge that our forefathers, many of them, found that mercy with the Lord because we know by those monuments of piety that they left behind them, that they had the zeal of God in them; which is a good ground of hope, as we may see. It was Paul's hearty desire and prayer to God for Israel that they might be saved, because they had the "zeal of God," (Romans 10:1-2). 4. Say the Papists could certainly prove that our ancestors did both live and die Papists, yet is it no undutifulness in us, to swerve from their example in that in which we are sure they swerved from the word of God. And we are often charged in the Scripture not to make the example of our forefathers the rule of our conscience in this case, as we have heard.

3. For discovering the weak foundations that most Papists have to build their conscience on in the matter of their religion, which is no more but this, that their parents and ancestors were of that faith. And, this is not something only for Papists, but even the greatest part of ignorant people have no other ground for many things they hold in religion but only that it was the custom of their neighbors, and of their forefathers.

4. For the convincing of popery to be a false religion, even by their own argument, that it is a new doctrine, and has no true antiquity to commend it to us. 1. We are well able to show that many of their errors were

not received into the church for 600 years after Christ. We are able to name the first authors of many of their corruptions. 2. Though we could not prove they sprung up since the Apostles times, nor name the time when they first were broached, it would not follow from there, that their religion is the faith that was first delivered by the Apostles. For 1. Many heresies began in the Apostle's days, (1 John 2:18 and 4:1). Yes, it is said that popery began to work then, (2. Thess. 2:7). 2. It is often noted in the word of sundry spirits of error, that they use to creep in so privily, that they cannot easily be spied or discerned, (Matt. 13:25; Gal. 2:4; 2 Tim. 3:6; 2 Peter 2:1; Jude 1:4). And above all heresies Popery is called a mystery, (2 Thess. 2:7). It is no wonder, therefore, that men could not discern when first it began to work. 3. There are many gross errors that have been held in the church (as the Papists themselves will confess) the first author of which cannot be named. 4. The reason is evident why the errors of popery were not easily discerned at first, nor opposed, because they (many of them especially) carried such a great show of holiness and were (happily) first broached by such as were esteemed holy and good men, (1 Timothy 4:3), and yet, they teach lies through hypocrisy. 3. Though we had no other reason to prove their religion to be new, this is sufficient, that it is not grounded on the holy Scriptures.

CHAPTER 5:
HEARING CHRIST

"Jesus saith unto her, Woman, believe me, the hour cometh, when ye shall neither in this mountain, nor yet at Jerusalem, worship the Father. Ye worship ye know not what: we know what we worship: for salvation is of the Jews. But the hour cometh, and now is, when the true worshippers shall worship the Father in spirit and in truth: for the Father seeketh such to worship him," (John 4:21-23).

These words contain the answer that our Savior gives to that question and doubt which the woman of Samaria had propounded to him in the former verse. Her question was (as we have seen) concerning the place of God's worship; yet not concerning the place of God's moral worship; (for she knew well enough, that the Jews used to pray, and to read, and preach; not in Jerusalem only, but in all their synagogues). But her question was, concerning the *place* of God's solemn worship, which stood in sacrifices and other ceremonies, appointed in Moses Law; which the Jews held might be performed only in Jerusalem; the Samaritans only in the temple they had upon mount Gerizim. This she (being ignorant and superstitious) esteemed to be the only worship of God. And concerning the place where this worship was to be performed, she desires to be resolved by our Savior Christ. Our Savior's answer to her question consists of two parts. First, concerning the place of God's worship, which she desired to be resolved in, and that is set down in verse 21. The second concerns the worship itself, which she did so highly esteemed, and that is set down in the three verses following. The sum of the first part of his answer, which is contained in this 21st verse, (and concerns the place of God's worship) is this: that though the time had been that the Jews (by good warrant of God's word) had held Jerusalem and the temple there, and the Samaritans (out of their superstition) had held mount Gerezim and the temple there, holier than any other place in the world besides, and that the worship done there (even for the place's sake) was more acceptable to God then if it had been done in any other place; yet, the time was "now at hand," that all difference of places for God's worship should be taken away, and this partition-wall that was between the Jews, and the Samaritans, and all other nations, should be broken down. Therefore, there was no cause that she should trouble herself about the place of God's worship, to know which of the two places was more holy, or the better to serve God in. And this he is not content barely to affirm, but confirms it to her by a vehement asseveration, "Woman, believe me, this is so."

For the interpretation of these words, and clearing them from all obscurity, we must observe the following. 1. That by the hour he speaks of here, he means the just time and moment that God in his eternal counsel had set for the abrogation of the ceremonial Law; and that was the time of his death, and passion, when so soon as he had said, John 19:30, "It is finished." "He gave up the ghost, and presently the veil of the temple was rent from the top to the bottom, (Matt. 27:51). From that hour there was no more holiness in the temple then in any other place.

2. By saying the "hour commeth," and not "shall come," his meaning is to note that it should come presently. So, Micah 7:4, "The day of thy watchmen and thy visitation commeth." So Psalm 37:13, "he seeth that his day is coming."

3. That when he says, "they shall worship God, neither in this mount, nor at Jerusalem," his meaning is not, that it should be unlawful after his death, to worship God, in either of those places. For the apostles and the rest of the faithful, did, after his death, and ascension "continue daily with one accord in the temple," (Acts 2:46). But his meaning is, they should not do it only there, nor be addicted to those places, more than to any other.

4. When Christ says, "ye shall neither in this mount, nor at Jerusalem," *etc.* speaking to one person in the plural number, he means all such as desired to serve God rightly (as this poor woman now did) intimating also in this, that this woman should become a true Christian, a true worshipper of God.

5. When he says by *the Father*, is not meant the first person in the Trinity (as if our worship and prayers were only to be directed to him) but the whole Godhead. As is seen in 1 Cor. 8:6, "There is but one God, which is the Father," or Eph. 4:6, "One God and Father of all, which is above all, and through all, and in you all." The reason why God is called *the Father*, are the following. 1. Because he is the fountain of our being, and of our whole welfare. As in Mal. 2:10, "Have we not one Father? Hath not one God made us?" 2. Because this, of all names, is most fit to allure us to worship him, and call on him. As soon as God's Spirit makes us able to pray, he teaches us to cry "Abba Father," (Gal. 4:6). And our Savior, of all the

names and attributes of God, teaches us to call him by *that* name, when we would pray to him, (Matt. 6:9). 3. In this place, most specially, he calls him the Father, rather than God, to meet with the superstitious conceit this woman had of her fathers; and to teach her, that in matters of her conscience and religion, only one Father is to be acknowledged, even the Lord, according to Matt. 23:9, "Call no man your Father upon earth, for one is your Father which is in heaven."

These words interpreted in this way divide themselves into two parts.

1. The assertion by which he confirms and seeks to persuade this woman in the doctrine that he teaches in these words, "Woman believe me."

2. The *doctrine* itself which he teaches, and confirms to her by this emphatic assertion, "The hour commeth, when ye shall neither in this mountain, nor at Jerusalem worship the Father." Now that we may receive instruction from the first part; it is to be observed here, that our Savior is teaching this woman a great point of doctrine. It touches on the abrogation of the law of Moses, and of the temple. This is a point he had not taught before to anyone, as being a doctrine indeed which the Jews were not fit to hear. He uses no proof and authority to confirm it to her but his own bare testimony, "Woman believe me," as if he should have said, "do not rest on your conscience or on the example of your forefathers, nor of your neighbors. Do not give credit to them in this case. Instead, believe me, and give credit to me."

From this we learn this DOCTRINE: This honor is due to Christ, and to him alone to be believed in matters of doctrine on his own word. None of all the prophets dare challenge this to themselves, but as they that did not come in their own name, but were only messengers from another. They were interpreters of the will of another, and they always delivered their doctrine under this warrant, "Thus saith the Lord," (Jer. 2:2; Ezek. 2:4). Nor any of the Apostles did this on their own testimony. Whatever Paul taught, he was accustomed to confirm it by authority of the written word, (Acts 28:23). He preached to them out of the law of Moses, and out of the Prophets. They did not desire that anything should be received into the church on their credit, but they carefully shunned this as a high presumption. This was the way the Prophets spoke, Isaiah 21:10, "That which I have heard of the Lord of hosts, the God of Israel, have I showed unto you." And this was what the Apostle Paul said in 1 Cor. 11:23, "I have received of the Lord, that which I have delivered unto you." And on the other hand, we shall find that our Savior taught after another fashion, not as an interpreter of the law, but as the law-giver himself, Luke 4:32, "They were astonied at his doctrine, for his word was with power," and Matt. 7:29, "He taught as one having authority, and not as the Scribes; nor as any other teachers were accustomed to do." Indeed, he often confirms his doctrine by Scripture, (John 6:45; Luke 19:46, and 24:46). He did this, 1. Either in respect of their weakness, whom he instructed; because they did not so fully know him to be the Son of God, but the testimony of the Scripture was of more authority with them, "I receive not the testimony of man (he says, John 5:34) but these things I say that ye may be saved." Therefore, he alleged the Scripture is called their law, (John 8:17 and 10:34 and

15:25). Or 2. To confirm to them the authority of the Scriptures, and to give us an example. But that was more than he was bound to do, or then he was accustomed usually to do. Therefore, this was the usual confirmation he gave of his doctrine. John 3:3, 5, "Verily, verily I say unto you." And against all the false interpretations of the law of God that had been delivered by the ancient fathers, he opposes no more but his own authority, "ye have heard that it was said thus and thus to them of old time. But I say unto you, thus and thus," (Matt. 5:22).

There are two reasons for the doctrine. 1. The reason why our Savior was to be believed on his bare word, is, because even as he was man, there was no sin nor error in him, 1 Peter 2:22, "He did no sin, neither was there guile found in his mouth." But, Christ, he was more than man, he was God himself. He was the Author of the whole word of God, which is therefore called the "word of Christ," (Col. 3:16), and therefore he did not need to confirm anything by Scripture. Every word he spoke, was the word of God, and therefore, credit was due to it by right, without any further proof. It was he that said, Prov. 8:8, "All the words of my mouth are righteous."

2. The reason why no man's word is to be taken in matters of doctrine, or religion, is this; because all men are subject to error, (1 Cor. 13:9). There is imperfection in our knowledge, and imperfection in our prophesying and teaching of others, (Romans 3:4). Let God be true, and every man a liar. This is proper to God, that he cannot be deceived himself, nor deceive others. And God's people would have been in great danger, in giving too much credit and authority even to very good men, as we may see in these three examples. First, that of the old Prophet, 1

Kings 13:18; that of Peter, Gal. 2:13; and that of the brethren, who dissuaded Paul from going to Jerusalem, (Acts 21:12).

This doctrine serves both for exhortation, and for reproof.

The first *use* is to exhort every one of us, to give this glory to Christ, as to believe him on his word, to give credit to the word of God, even without the testimony or authority of any man. Yes, though we see no reason for it, or yes, though it seems never so contrary to our own reason. When once we hear, "Thus saith the Lord," this must suffice for us, instead of all reason. Here we must rest and satisfy ourselves. This is called the obedience of faith, (Romans 16:26). Yes, this is the first and chief obedience that God requires of us. The first work of his grace in us, is to subdue our reason, (2 Cor. 10:5), "Casting down the imaginations, and bringing into captivity every thought to the obedience of Christ." Until we have attained to this simplicity, we shall never become wise to salvation, nor come to any comfortable certainty in the matters of religion. This is that simplicity which is spoken of in Psalm 19:7. "The testimony of the Lord is sure, and giveth wisdom to the simple," and Prov. 1:4, "To give unto the simple sharpness of wit."

The second *use* of this doctrine is to dissuade us from giving that honor to any man, as to receive any thing in religion on his word or credit. For this honor as you have heard, belongs to Christ alone. The Apostle requires indeed, that God's people should obey them that have the oversight of them, and subject themselves, (Heb. 13:17). But this obedience is not such as the Jesuits bind themselves and their scholars to, absolute obedience, to receive and believe everything that they teach. But there is liberty and commandment also given to all God's people, to *try* the doctrine of their teachers, whether it is agreeable to the word of God or not; and accordingly, to receive or reject it. You know that the Bereans are commended for doing this, though they had no meaner teachers then Paul and Silas, (Acts 17:11). And it was to the people, that that commandment was given, 1 Thess. 5:20, "Despise not prophesyings, prove all things," and 1 John 4:1, "believe not every spirit, but try the spirits whether they be of God."

The third *use* of this doctrine is for reproof. For there are many that give too little credit to Christ, and too much to man.

1. The Papists give every bit as much credit to the church, as they do to the word of God; no, even more a great deal. They will not believe the Scripture, unless the church gives testimony to it. But they will believe the church even in those things, in which the Scripture gives no testimony to it at all. Let the Scripture teach anything never so plainly, never so clearly, they will still doubt of its meaning. And how do you know this to be the meaning they say? As if the Scriptures (of which the Holy Spirit says, Romans 15:4, "Whatsoever is written, is written for our learning," and 2 Tim. 3:16, "The whole Scripture is profitable to instruction," even if they were uttered, and written like Apollos' oracles, so darkly, as none could have any certainty of their meaning. On the other hand, let the church hold anything, even if it is absurd, and contrary to religion and to reason as well, yet, they may not question anything of it. So that to them, without a doubt that curse belongs to them, Jer. 17:5,

"Cursed be the man that trusteth in man, and maketh flesh his arm, and withdraweth his heart from the Lord."

2. The disputer of the world, of whom the Apostle speaks, 1 Cor. 1:20, "Where is the disputer of this world?" the one who will receive no more in religion then they can see reason for. Scripture will not serve their turn, for they must have a reason. Such as give liberty to themselves, not only nourish their own hearts with many reasonings and oppositions against such truths, but this rebellion is manifestly taught in the holy Scripture. Who would dare to openly reason, and maintain an argument against the word of God? 1. I do not blame anyone for asking, doubting, or making question of the meaning of such places of Scripture, as are obscure, (as some places indeed are, 2 Peter 3:16). For the disciples asked questions in Mark 4:20 and are not reproved for it. But I blame those people who dare reason against such places of Scripture, as are plain and manifest. 2. I do not deny, but a Christian may desire to know the reason of what he holds and believes in religion, and of whatsoever is taught him. He does this with 1. reverence, 2. out of a desire to be further confirmed in the truth, 3. with a resolution to yield to that reason which God has revealed in his word, and to seek no further. For every one should be able to answer them that demand a reason of him of the hope that is in him, (1 Peter 3:15). And Christians should seek to be not children, but of a ripe age in knowledge, (1 Cor. 14:20). And the blessed Virgin is not blamed for asking with this mind, "How can this be?" (Luke 1:34). But it is a dangerous sin, not to rest in the authority of the Scripture; not to *count it*, as the idea of resting means in this. Let every man take heed how he gives himself liberty

to cavil and dispute against such truths, as are clearly revealed in the Scripture; that is that which the Apostle so reproves in Romans 9:19-20, speaking of the high mystery of God's predestination, "Thou wilt say then unto me, why doth he yet find fault? for who hath resisted his will? Nay, but O man who art thou that repliest against God?" Those things which we cannot understand, we must admire, and say, as the Apostle does, Romans 11:33, "O the depth," *etc.* Laying the fault not upon the Scriptures, but on our own stupidity and inability to conceive reason for it. For there are many truths of God revealed in the word, which are such mysteries, as it is not possible for man by reason, and by light of nature to conceive. No, indeed the whole doctrine of the Gospel is in this way, "so, we speak the wisdom in a mystery," the Apostle says in 1 Cor. 2:7. And in 1 Tim. 3:16, "Great is the mystery of godliness," yes, the more a man excels in natural reason and understanding, the more unable shall he be to conceive them, for Romans 8:17, "The wisdom of the flesh is enmity to God." It is God only, by that supernatural light of his Spirit, which he reveals these things, (Matt. 16:17). And God will not reveal it to anyone but to those that are meek and humble, to none that have such high conceit of themselves, and attribute so much to their own reason. Psalm 25:9, "the meek will he teach his way."

3. The curious hearer that disdains that ministry, as unlearned, and of no worth, that brings no other authority, nor other testimonies, but the testimony of the word of God; and yet it is evident, this was the course that the Prophets and Apostles, yes, and Christ himself took in their ministry. 2. The Scripture is sufficient to

every purpose that concerns the ministry, even to make men wise to salvation; to teach, to convince, to reprove, to exhort, and even to make the man of God (the Minister of God) perfect, thoroughly furnished to every good work that he has to do in the whole exercise of his ministry, (2 Tim. 3:15-17). 3. There is no such certainty in any other testimony as the conscience can rely on, because every man is subject to error, (Romans 3:4).

4. The careless hearer, that never examines what he hears, but receives everything upon the credit of such as teach him. It is the commandment of Christ, Mark 4:24, "Take heed what you hear." And it is too much readiness in receiving that which is taught to us, if we receive it before we have examined it, (Acts 17:11). It is said to be a property of a fool to believe everything, (Prov. 14:15). Yes, it is noted for the misery of a natural man, that (like a beast) he is carried away as he is lead, (2 Cor. 12:2). Three benefits Christians should find in this, if they would examine by the word whatsoever they hear, and labor to see the ground of it in the Scripture, before they receive it.

1. They should grow to certainty in what they hold, when their faith shall not stand in the wisdom of men, but of the power of God, as the Apostle speaks in 1 Cor. 2:5. So the other cannot.

2. They would persevere, and hold fast what they have learned, Matt. 13:44, for when he had withdrawn himself, and examined the treasure, he sold everything for it. Contrarily, he that incontinently and over-hastily received the word, was soon gone, (Matt. 13:21).

3. They would obey, and make a conscience practice of what they know, and the other kind of man

cannot. For the when the Apostle speaks of the obedience of the Thessalonians, and of the power his ministry had in their hearts and lives, he gives this for a reason, 1 Thess. 2:13, "that they received the word of God which they heard of him, not as the word of man, but as it was indeed the word of God, which also did work effectually in them that believed." For then would the doctrine be mighty in operation, when it is once found to be well grounded on the word, of which it is said, Heb. 4:12, that it is lively and mighty in operation.

CHAPTER 6:
CHRIST'S DEATH AND WORSHIP

In the last chapter we learned that this verse contains the first part of Christ's answer to the question that this woman propounded to him, and that it consists of two parts. 1. An emphatic assertion by which he confirms the doctrine that he was to teach her in these words, "Woman believe me." 2. The doctrine itself in these words, "The hour commeth," *etc.* We have finished the assertion and so now we come to the doctrine itself.

The words I interpreted to you, and told you their meaning, was this: that the time was then at hand (namely the time of his Passion) when all those who desired to worship God aright (as this woman did) should not stand more addicted to, or put more holiness in Mount Gerizim (or Jerusalem either) then in any other place. So that the *doctrine* we are to learn from these words, is this: that this is one benefit we have by the death of our Savior, that now all religious difference concerning the place of worship is taken away; no one place is holier then another.

Before I confirm this doctrine, I will clear it from an objection that may be made against it. One might say, "If all difference of places is taken away, then it seems a man may serve God in his workshop, or chamber as well as in the church." I answer. 1. Our Savior does not compare private places with public; but public with public, private with private. 2. It is true indeed, there is more respect to be had, and more good to be received by the service that is done to God in the church, then by that which is done in any private house. For the Apostle speaks of this as of a fearful sin, and step to the unpardonable sin, to forsake the assemblies, the gathering of ourselves together, μὴ ἐγκαταλείποντες τὴν ἐπισυναγωγὴν ἑαυτῶν, καθὼς ἔθος τισίν, (Heb. 10:25-26). But that makes the service which we do to God better in the assembly than that which we can do to him in our house. But, it is not the place that has any holiness in it, but the assembly with which we join.

1. In the public assembly we have the help of the ministry of the word and sacraments, the use of which is to inflame and kindle devotion in our hearts. "Did not our hearts burn within us while he talked with us, and while he opened to us the Scriptures," the disciples said, (Luke 24:32). It is there in the midst of the assembly and the preaching of the word where God's Spirit conveys grace into us, and is therefore called "the ministration of the spirit," (2 Cor. 3:8).

2. We have the example of the zeal and devotion, and cheerfulness of others of God's servants, with whom we join. This is of great force to correct our own sluggishness and drowsiness, and to quicken God's graces in us, "Your zeal provoked many," Paul says in 2 Cor. 9:2. And David professes that he received "much good," by beholding the forwardness of the rest of God's people, in "frequenting the house of God," (Psalm 122:1-2). And I do not doubt, but very many wicked men have found in their own experience, that as it is said of Saul, when he came among the prophets, though he came even with evil mind, yet another heart was given him. The Spirit of God came on him also, and he became like one of them, (1 Sam. 19:23-24). So, these men in the assembly of God's people,

by beholding the reverent attention and devotion of others, have found many good motions worked in themselves.

3. There is much more force in the prayers, in which many of God's servants join together, then there can be in those, that any of them shall make severally and apart. The joined forces of many must necessarily prevail more with God, then if they were single. Prayer therefore is compared to "seeking" and "knocking," (Matt. 7:7). And when many seek a thing, there is more hope of finding. When many knock at heaven's gates, they will be better heard, (Matt. 18:19). "Verily I say unto you that if two of you (*much more if many*) shall agree on earth upon any thing, whatsoever they shall desire, it shall be given them of my Father which is in heaven." See the force of public prayer, in which many of God's servants join together. Therefore, God's people at such times as they have most desired to prevail with God in prayer, have been careful to gather together, as public assemblies, as they possibly could.

4. Christ has promised to be present in a more special and comfortable manner in the assemblies of his people, then in any of our houses, or in any other place, (Matt. 18:20 and 28:20). So that (for the assembly's sake) the service we do to God in the church, is to be preferred before that which we can do in any other place; not for any holiness that is in the place itself.

And there we have the clearing of the doctrine from the objection that might be made against it. Now I come to its confirmation. And to this purpose we must observe a notable difference in this case, between the time before the death of our Savior Christ, and that which followed.

Before our Savior's death we shall read of diverse places, that were holier than others. 1. The whole land of Canaan, (because it was a type of the church of Christ, and of the kingdom of heaven) was esteemed by God's people a better and more holy place than any other in the world. That (among other reasons) made Jacob and Joseph to be so desirous to be buried there. Five things are worthy to be observed in Jacob's desire of this. He desired to be buried in Canaan though, 1. It was a great way off. 2. It could not be without great offence. Of Jacob we read he calls Joseph, and charges him, (Gen. 47:2, 31). And not content with that, he charges all his sons with it, (Gen. 49:29). 2. When? immediately before his death; as a matter that he had the greatest care of, (Gen. 47:29). 3. In what manner? Exceeding affectionately and earnestly, (Gen. 47:29). "If I have found grace in thy sight, deal mercifully and truly with me, bury me not I pray thee in Egypt." 4. He bound his good son Joseph by oath to it, and would not take his word, (Gen. 47:29, 31). 5. When he had gotten Joseph to swear, his heart was so comforted, that he gave solemn thanks to God for it, (Genesis 47:31).

2. In the land of Canaan, some places are said to have been more holy then others: namely such, as where God manifested himself in a special and sensible manner. So the place where the Son of God appeared to Moses in the fiery bush, is called "holy ground," (Exod. 3:5). And that in which he appeared to Joshua, (Joshua 5:15). And the Mount on which he was transfigured is called by Peter, the Holy Mount, (1 Peter 1:18). But these places

were no longer accounted holy, then during the time of this special presence of the Lord in them. Neither can we read that any of God's people went on a pilgrimage to those places after, or gave any religious respect to them.

3. Jerusalem, because it was the place that the Lord had chosen to put his name there, was ever (from the days of David to Christ's time) holier than any other place of the world beside. It is called the holy City, (Matt. 4:5), yes, even to the very moment of Christ's death it continued this way, notwithstanding its marvelous sins and corruptions, it is still called the holy City still, (Matt. 27:53).

4. The temple (because God had hallowed it to put his name there forever, 2 Chron. 7:16) was yet a more holy place than any other place in Jerusalem, and is therefore often called, the holy temple, (Psalm 5:8). Five things are noted that show the temple to have been a most holy place. 1). God's people were bound wherever they dwelt, to resort there at certain times, three times every year all the males were bound to appear there, (Exod. 23:17). The Eunuch you know came even from Ethiopia to worship there, (Acts 8:27). 2). Many parts of God's worship they might perform nowhere else, but only there, "thither shall ye bring all that I command you, your burnt offerings, and your sacrifices, your tithes, and the heave offering of your hand, and all the choice vows, which ye vow unto the Lord," (Deut. 12:11). 3). Those parts of God's service which they might perform in other places, (as prayer, even private prayer) was much better and more pleasing to God, and more available to their comfort there than in any other place. In which respect it is called, Matt. 21:12, "the house of prayer." And 2 Chron.

7:15, "Mine eyes shall be open, and mine ears attentive to the prayer made in this place." Therefore, David desired to behold God's power and glory, as he had beheld it in the sanctuary, (Psalm 63:1-2). Therefore it is said of Anna, that (though through the affliction of her mind, she could not partake with her husband in the sacrifice and offerings) yet she went up with him duly to the house of the Lord, even to make her secret prayers there, (1 Samuel 1:12). She continued praying before the Lord. David went there to make his private prayers, (2 Sam. 7:18). So did the good publican, (Luke 18:10). Yes, 4). When they could not go there to pray, yet just looking towards the temple, made their prayer more acceptable with God, according to that prayer Solomon made in the dedication of the temple that it might be so, (1 Kings 8:44, 48). 5). Yes, so holy was that temple, and it had such religious reverence from God's people to bear to it, that after the Chaldeans had burned it, they honored the very place where it had stood, and esteemed it holier than any other. This appears by those 80 people whom Ishmael murdered, (Jer. 41:5). And by Daniel's action in opening his windows towards Jerusalem when he prayed, (Dan. 6:10).

5. In the temple itself, though all the parts of it were holy, yet some places in it were more holy then others. For there was a place, where the people stood separated from the priests, (Luke 1:10). And this was a holy place, so holy, that Mark 11:16 says Christ would not allow any to carry any vessel through it. And there was a place where the priests executed their ministry, which was holier than that, that the people stood in, and is therefore called *the holy place*, (Lev. 16:30). And there was a place which the high Priest might only enter into, and

that but once a year, and that is called the holy of holies, the holiest place of all, (Heb. 9:3). Now since the death of Christ, there is no place of the world, holier than another. No nation is holy as the Land of Canaan was, no town as Jerusalem, no place where God is worshipped, as the temple was. Prayer is as available with God in one place as in another. 1. Private prayer is as in 1 Cor. 1:2 where Paul describes the faithful to be such as call on God in every place. 2. Public prayer is this way, 1. Tim. 2:8, "I will that men pray every where." 3. Generally the whole worship of God is this way, Matt. 18:2, "Wheresoever two or three are gathered together in my name," *etc.* And this the Lord foretold to his prophets, as a singular privilege, that should come to the church in the days of the Gospel, (Zeph. 2:11). Every man in all the parts of the nations, shall worship God from his own place. Malachi 1:11 says that in every place from the rising of the sun, to the "going down thereof, incense shall be offered unto my name, and a pure offering" (incense and offering are named as the service that was peculiar unto the temple). Isaiah 19:19, "In that day shall the Altar of the Lord be in the midst of Egypt, and a pillar by the border thereof." And if this privilege was promised to Egypt, which of all nations had most of all provoked God, how much more to other nations?

To make this truth the more evident to the world, as the veil of the temple was torn immediately upon Christ's death, so within forty years after, (when by the Apostles ministry this doctrine was sufficiently manifested to the world) the temple and city were utterly subverted and overthrown, according to the prophecy of Christ, Luke 19:44, "They shall make thee even with the ground, and not leave in thee a stone upon a stone." And Daniel 9:26 long before prophesied that the Romans should destroy both the city and the sanctuary.

The *reasons* of this great alteration and change, why this great difference took place, that was in places before, is now quite taken away; why Jerusalem and the temple lost all that holiness that was in them before, are principally four reasons:

1. Because by Christ's coming (and specially by his death) all that was fulfilled, that was signified by the temple. For the temple was but a type and shadow of Christ's humanity, as our Savior himself witnesses, (John 2:21). And the proportion stands in two points. 1). As the Lord dwelt in the temple, and his glory sensibly appeared in it, (1 Kings 8:11), so all the fullness of the God-head did dwell bodily, and personally in Christ, (Col. 2:9). 2). As no sacrifice was acceptable to God, unless it were offered in the temple, So none of our prayers, and spiritual sacrifices, are acceptable to God, unless they are offered up to God in Christ, (1 Peter 2:5). So that it is necessary, that when the body was come, the shadow should cease.

2. Since Christ's death, all difference of people is taken away; and all nations are as acceptable to God, as the Jews were, (Acts 10:34-35). Of this truth I perceive, "God is no accepter of persons: but in every nation, he that feareth God and worketh righteousness," is accepted of him. Gal. 3:28, "For there is neither Jew nor Grecian, bond nor free, male nor female: for ye are all one in Christ." And therefore, any difference in any place must necessarily also be taken away. For this difference of places, was as a partition-wall, between the Jews and all the Gentiles. "For he is our peace, who hath made both

one, and hath broken down the middle wall of partition between us; Having abolished in his flesh the enmity, even the law of commandments contained in ordinances; for to make in himself of twain one new man, so making peace," (Eph. 2:14).

3. The grievous sins, by which Jerusalem, and the temple were defiled, caused God to destroy and profane it; and of the most holy and honorable place, to make it the most miserable and abominable of all the places of the world. For the profanation of the temple, our Savior tells them, they should see, Matt. 24:15, the abomination of desolation (that is an abominable desolation) stand in the holy place. No place was ever destroyed in the same way. Accordingly, the Lord said in Jer. 26:9, "I will make this place as Shilo, and this city a curse to all the inhabitants of the earth. It was such a miserable destruction, that our Savior says in Luke 23:30, they should cry "to the mountains, fall on us, and to the hills, cover us." And this is reckoned to be its cause, Matt. 23:37-38, "Jerusalem, Jerusalem, which killest the Prophets, and stonest them that are sent to thee. How often would I have gathered thy children together, as the Hen gathereth her chickens under her wings, and ye would not? Behold your habitation shall be left unto you desolate."

4. The Lord has not, since the destruction of the temple and city of Jerusalem, sanctified any other place in the world, or consecrated it to a more holy use then the rest; and it is only God's institution and word that can make anything or any place holy. Every creature and ordinance of God is sanctified by the word of God and prayer, (1 Tim. 4:5). Nothing can be sanctified but by the word and prayer. The Sabbath is a holier day then all the

rest because the Lord by his institution sanctified it, (Exod. 20:11). The water in baptism is holy, because the Lord in his word has consecrated it to that holy use. God "sanctifieth and cleanseth us with the washing of water by the word," (Eph. 5:26). The bread and wine in the Lord's Supper are holy, because the Lord appointed them to be used in that holy action. He took bread and wine, and after he had blessed them by his prayer and thanksgiving, used them in this holy action as signs of his body and blood, and seals of the New Covenant, (Matt. 26:26-27; Luke 22).

The *use* of this doctrine is threefold. 1. To reprove various superstitions of the Papists, and of ignorant people, that have by tradition received it from the Papists. 1). Their going on pilgrimage to the holy Land, (as they call it) and to other places which by reason of some relics of saints that are said to be there, are accounted more holy than any other places. This is counted a chief work of piety, and devotion among them. There are *Five Reasons* against this superstition. 1]. Nothing can make a place, or anything else holy, but the ordinance and institution of God, as we have heard. 2]. Of all places, Jerusalem now does not deserve the name of the Holy Land. For Numbers 35:33, blood defiles the Land; and in it was the blood of all the prophets and of Christ himself shed, (Matt. 23:37). 3]. The relics of saints, which they pretend make those places holier, are notoriously known to be counterfeit. 4]. If the true bodies of the saints were indeed there, yet such religious respect should not be given to those places for them. For, for this cause the place where Moses was buried (even under the Law when some places were holier than others) was so carefully concealed, lest the people of God should give religious respect to it, (Deut. 34:6). Yes, even Michael the archangel strove, and disputed with the devil about this point in Jude 1. 5]. It is Judaism and a denial of Christ to come or to hold that one place is holier than another, as is evident by our text.

2. The second superstition of Papists reproved by this doctrine is that they put more holiness in some places of burial, then in others. For they hold, that it is more beneficial to the dead, to be buried in the church-yard, then out of it; and in the church more than in the church-yard; and in the chancel more than in the church; and near the high altar, more than in any other place of the chancel; and that on this conceit, that these places are consecrated and hallowed; that they are holier than other places are. 1]. I do not deny, but a Christian may lawfully desire to be buried in the place where the rest of the faithful are buried. 2]. There may be more civil honor done to some Christians then to others, even in the place of their burial. It was a honor lawfully done to Hezekiah, that he was buried in the chief of the sepulchers of the sons of David, (2 Chron. 32:33). But to put any holiness in this "thing," or to think the place where one is buried can any way tend to the benefit of the dead, that is gross superstition, and is most unlawful. 3]. The third superstition condemned by this doctrine is that they hold private prayer made in a church more available, because the church says there is a more holy place than another. Where it is evident by what has been said, that our houses and chambers are in themselves, as holy places, as the churches are. That private and secret prayer are fitter places then any church. "When thou prayest enter into thy closet, and when thou hast shut the door, pray to thy

Father which is in secret," (Matt. 6:6). 4]. The fourth superstition condemned by this doctrine is, that they put holiness and religion even in the situation of their temples, and placing of their bodies in prayer. For the temple (they say) should be built towards the east, and we should worship towards the east. Where, it is not religiously material which way our churches stand, or which way we turn ourselves in prayer except that our hearts are lifted up and directed to our Father which is in heaven. Yet if any part of heaven is more unfit for us to turn our faces towards in prayer than another, the east is the most unfit. There we find idolaters blamed for doing this, Ezekiel 8:16, which we cannot find noted of any other part. Though the matter itself is of a small matter, yet to put *holiness in it*, is a great sin, as is evident by that bitter invective our Savior makes against the Pharisees and Jews for the holiness they put in washing their hands and cups and such things, (Mark 7:6, 9).

The second use of this doctrine is to exhort us, that since we have learned that this is one chief privilege we have by Christ's death, that all religious difference of any places is taken away, and our nation now is as holy as Canaan, our towns as Jerusalem, our houses as the temple, then, we should therefore make use of this privilege in serving God, not in our temples only, but in our houses also. We should establish the exercises of religion in our families, and use them there constantly and conscionably. We read of Abraham, that wherever he pitched his tent he was accustomed to erect an altar to God, (Gen. 12:8 and 13:18). And many Christians are said to have had churches in their houses, (Romans 16:5; Col. 4:15; Philemon 2). Under the Law they were accustomed to dedicate their houses, and consecrate them to God before they dwelt in them, (Deut. 20:5; Psalm 30 in its entirety). Though this were done then with sundry ceremonies, which are now abolished, yet the equity remains, and we also should dedicate our houses to God. We can do that in no better way than this, 2 Sam. 6:11, "God blessed the house of Obed-Edom, while the Ark was entertained in it." And how can this choice but bring a blessing from God on our dwellings if he were served constantly in them? Contrarily, Jer. 10:25, there is a prophetical imprecation against those families, in which no prayer is used.

The third use of this doctrine is to teach us, that such is the severity of God against sin, that he will not only plague them that commit it, but curse the very place where it has been committed. Jerusalem and the House of God may be an example to all places in the world in this point. For what places in the world had so many privileges as Jerusalem and the temple there? Of which it is said, 2 Chron. 7:16, "I have now chosen and sanctified this place, that my name may be there forever: and mine eyes and mine heart shall be there perpetually." And Lam. 4:12, "The Kings of the earth, and all the inhabitants of the world would not have believed, that the adversary and the enemy, should have entered into the gates of Jerusalem," and yet behold how the sins committed in it, made it the most accursed place in the world. It is a special blessing often promised to the godly, that their habitation and dwelling shall prosper, (Prov. 3:33). That he will make the habitation of their righteousness prosperous, (Job 8:6). Yes, that they shall know and feel, that peace shall be in their tabernacles (Job 5:24), and about them, and their houses, and all that they have. God keeps such a fence as Satan cannot hurt them, (Job 1:10). It is the protection of God alone that keeps our houses from the calamities of fire within, and lightning from heaven, and from the annoyance and molestation of evil spirits, and other judgments. On the other hand it is certain, the curse of God is on the habitation of the wicked, (Prov. 3:33 and 14:11). The house of the wicked shall be overthrown. Sin defiles the house where it is committed, and brings God's curse on it. The houses on whose roofs idolatry had been committed "shall be set on fire, saith the Lord," (Jer. 32:29). The curse shall enter into the house of the thief, and of him that swears falsely, and "it shall remain in the midst of it, and it shall consume it with the timber thereof and the stones thereof," (Zech. 5:4). "It shall dwell in his tabernacle, because it is none of his: brimstone shall be scattered upon his habitation," (Job. 18:15). O that men would believe this! Then would victualers, either not endure such swearing, uncleanness, and drunkenness in their houses; or if they could not avoid it (living in that calling) they would give it over. Then masters of families would be content to be free from swearing, drunkenness, and filthiness; but would put these sins far from their tabernacles also, as Eliphaz speaks, "thou shalt be built up, thou shalt put away iniquity far from thy tabernacles," (Job 22:23).

CHAPTER 7:
GOD REGULATES WORSHIP

We have already heard that the answer which our Savior makes to the question that this woman moved him to explain two parts. The first concerns the place of God's worship, which she desired to be resolved, and that is set down in the 21st verse. The second concerns the worship itself about which she moved her question; namely, the ceremonial worship that was offered to God in Jerusalem, and mount Gerizim. And this part of his answer is contained in this part of the verse as well as those two that follow it. The sum and effect of this part of his answer concerns the worship which the Jews offered to God being far better than that of the Samaritans. Yet, this ceremonial worship about which she is now so inquisitive, whether it were that, that the Jews used, or that which the Samaritans used, was not to be so esteemed, as she thought. Rather, it would shortly be abolished, and instead, another form of God's worship should be established which would not consist in ceremonies and shadows (that suited so well with our carnal and corrupt nature) but should be spiritual (as best agreeing with the nature of God) and should have in it the truth and substance of all that which was figured and shadowed in those ceremonies. So that these three verses divide themselves into two parts, 1. A commendation of that outward worship of God, that the Jews used in comparison of that of the Samaritans, and that is set down in this verse. 2. A discommendation of that outward worship of God, that the Jews used in comparison of that, which God would shortly establish in his church; and that is contained in the two verses following.

In this verse, he commends the religion and worship of God that the Jews used and prefers it before that of the Samaritans, by this argument; because the Samaritans worshipped "they knew not what." But the Jews did not do this, and he proves this because "salvation was of the Jews." The obscurity that is in any of these words, I will clear, and interpret it, as I come to the handling of the doctrines that arise out of them. 1. We are to observe here that our Savior says "they worshipped they knew not what." How could that be, seeing: 1). They knew that they worshipped the true God, even the same God that the Jews did. For they say this to Zerubbabel in Ezra 4:2, "We seek JEHOVAH your God as ye do." Yes, the Holy Spirit says of them in 2 Kings 17:3, "Thus they feared the Lord, and appointed priests, out of themselves for the high places, who prepared for them sacrifices in the house of the high places." 2). They knew what manner of worship they gave to him. For they offered sacrifices to him, (Ezra 4:2). They served him as they were taught and directed by one of the Priests that had served in Israel, before they were carried away captive by the Assyrians, (2 Kings 17:28). One of those Priests came and dwelt in Bethel, and taught them how they should serve the Lord. What then does our Savior mean to say, "they worshipped they knew not what?" Surely, because they did not know him by his word, they did not worship him according to his word. Therefore, they are said to worship "they know not what." This interpretation is grounded on what we shall find written in 2 Kings 17:34, "They did after the old manner," as verse 19, they neither "feared God, nor did after their ordinances, nor after their customs, nor after the Law, nor after the commandment which the Lord commanded the children of Jacob." On the other hand, because the Jews had the word of God, they knew God by his word, the worship they did to him, was appointed by his word. Therefore, are they said, to worship "what they knew." And this interpretation is further confirmed by the words that follow, "Salvation is of the Jews." What does Christ mean here by "salvation?" Surely the word, the doctrine and means of salvation, as it is also called in Heb. 2:5, "How shall we escape, if we neglect so great salvation." This was the chief prerogative the Jews had above others. So that these words, salvation is of the Jews, are the very same in effect with that which the Prophet Isaiah has said in, Isaiah 2:3, "The Law shall go from Zion, and the word of the Lord from Jerusalem."

So, the first doctrine we are to learn is this: that no man can know or serve God aright without the direction of his word. The doctrine has two branches. 1. No man can know God aright, nor conceive rightly of him, but by his word. 2. No man can serve or worship God aright, without the direction of his word. 1. The God which ignorant men and such as are not instructed by his word to serve, is not a true God, but an idol and imagination of their own. Psalm 76:1, "God is known in Judah." On the other hand, it is said of all natural men in Gal. 4:8, "But even then when ye knew not God, ye did service unto them, which by nature are not gods." So, it is said of the ten tribes in 2 Chron. 15:3, "Now for a long season Israel hath been without the true God, because they had been without a Priest to teach, and without the

Law." This is true, God makes himself known not to his church only by his word, but to all the world by his works. Men cannot open their eyes, or look any way, but they may see him in his works. Romans 1:20, "The invisible things of him, that is, his eternal power and God-head," are seen ever since the creation of the world, being considered in his works. Yes he says of all the Gentiles that (verse 21) "they knew God," and verse 19, "that which may be known of God is manifest in them," that is, in their hearts and consciences, for (he says) "God hath showed it unto them." So that there is no man living, but he has even by nature some knowledge of the true God in him. But this is not the true knowledge of God which should be a comfortable and saving knowledge of him.

Various notable differences may be observed between the knowledge of God, men attain to by the light of nature, or by the creatures, and that which is attained to by the word. 1. That serves to make men only without excuse, and cannot bring them to salvation, (Romans 1:20). But this is all-sufficient to make men wise to salvation, (2 Tim. 3:15), and therefore is called salvation here, and James 1:21 says it is said to be able to save the soul.

Secondly, that light is as a dim light, that knowledge is dark, obscure, and uncertain. By this knowledge they have of him by his creation and the light of nature, men have many strange conceits of God, and do not know what to think of him, (Romans 1:21). Though they knew God, yet they became vain in their imaginations, and their foolish hearts were full of darkness. But the word reveals God to us so clearly and so certainly, that the simplest may know him, Psalm 19:7, "The testimony of the Lord is sure, and giveth wisdom to the simple."

Thirdly, the knowledge of God that is gained by the creature, has no power to change and reform the heart. Romans 1:21, "When they knew God, they glorified him not as God, neither were thankful," but the knowledge of God that is gotten by the word, has power to convert the soul, (Psalm 19:7).

Fourthly, the knowledge of God that is gotten by other means, brings no comfort nor joy to the soul, but works in it rather a slavish fear of him. Eccl. 1:14, "I have seen all the works that are done under the sun; and behold all is vanity and vexation of spirit." And verse 18, "in much wisdom there is much grief, and he that increaseth knowledge increaseth sorrow." But, the knowledge of God we attain by the word rejoices the heart, so as the better we know him, the more comfort we have in him, (Psalm 19:8-10). So that you see now the first branch of the doctrine confirmed to you, that no man can know God aright, know him to his comfort, know him to his salvation but by his word.

The second branch of the doctrine shall be made as plain to you, that no man can worship God aright, but by the direction of his word. No service can please God, but that that is done by direction, and in obedience to his word. When the Lord had forbidden his people to serve him as the Canaanites had done, he adds in Deut. 12:32, "Whatsoever I command you, take heed you do it; thou shalt add nothing thereto, nor take ought there-from;" that is, do neither more nor less in my service then I have appointed. If we do something in his service which he has not forbidden, yet if he has not commanded it, we highly offend him, as is plain in the case of Nadab and Abihu, "They offered strange fire before the Lord which he commanded them not, and there went out fire from the Lord and devoured them," (Lev. 10:1-2). When the Tabernacle was to be built, Moses (though a wise and holy man) was not to be trusted with anything, but straightly charged, (Heb. 8:5). See "that thou make all things according to the pattern showed to thee in the Mount." This charge was repeated four times in Exod. 25:9, 40 and 26:30 and 27:28. And it is said when all was done, in Exod. 39:43, "Moses beheld that they had done all in every point as the Lord commanded, and he blessed them." So when mention is made that Solomon set the courses of the priests and singers, and of the porters for the House of God, lest we should think he did it of his own mind, his warrant is set down, and its expressly said, "For so was the commandment of David, the man of God," (2 Chron. 8:14). And yet more plainly, 2 Chron 29:25, when Hezekiah appointed the Levites to use in the church of God, cymbals, and viols, and harps, lest we should think he took on him to appoint anything in God's service, it is said, "He did it according to the commandment of David and Gad the Kings seer, and Nathan the Prophet." For the commandment was by the hand of the Lord, and by the hand of his prophets. See how precise God would have us to be in sticking close to the direction of his word, in the matter of his worship. Yes, it is certain, when we offer him any service, that he has not appointed us in his word, we do not serve him, but we serve an idol. This is plain here in the example of the Samaritans. They intended to worship the true God,

(2 Kings 17:32; Ezra 4:2), and yet it is said they did not worship the true God, (2 King. 17:34). What did they worship then? Surely an idol of their own brain. They worshipped "they knew not what." Why? Because they did not make the word the rule of their worship, but the custom of the country, (2 Kings 17:34, 40). Yes, while men think they serve the Lord, they serve the devil if the worship they offer to God is not grounded upon his word. This is plain in three examples.

1. It is certain, the Gentiles (as they had some knowledge of the true God, Romans 1:21) in all their superstitions they intended to worship him. For so Paul tells the Athenians, he preached no other God to them, but the same whom they did worship (Acts 17:23). Yet it is said of them in 1 Cor. 10:20, they worshipped devils and not God. Why? Because they worshipped him ignorantly, and not according to his word, (Acts 17:23). "they serve the unknown god."

2. Aaron and the Israelites intended to worship the true God in the similitude of the golden calf, as is plain in Psalm 106:20, "They changed their glory into the similitude of an ox that eateth grass." And Neh. 9:18, "This is the God (they said) that brought thee out of the land of Egypt," and Exod. 32:5, Aaron made an altar before it, and proclaimed, "Tomorrow shall be a holy day to JEHOVAH." And yet the Lord charges them for this that they had offered a burnt offering to the devil, Lev. 17:7.[17] Why? Because they were turned out of the way that he had commanded them, they swerved from the direction of

---

[17] "And they shall no more offer their sacrifices unto devils, after whom they have gone a whoring. This shall be a statute for ever unto them throughout their generations," (Lev. 17:7).

his word. Exod. 32:8, "They have turned quickly out of the way which I commanded."

3. The ten tribes intended to worship the true God when they erected the two calves, even the same God that was worshipped at Jerusalem. 1 Kings 22:28, "Behold O Israel thy gods," (that is, the similitude of thy gods) "that brought thee out of the land of Egypt." And yet the Holy Spirit says, "they served the devil," 2 Chron. 11:15, "He ordained him Priests for the high places, and for the devils, and for the calves that he made." And why? "Because they worshipped him not according to his word," (2 Chron. 15:3). Israel has been without the true God. Why? Because they were without a priest to teach them and without the Law.

The reasons of the doctrine are these. 1. For the first branch. No man knows the Father but the Son, and he to whom the Son will reveal him, (Matt. 11:27). And the means by which Christ reveals and makes his Father known to us is by the word. John 17:6, "I have declared thy name to the men that thou gavest me out of the world," verse 8, "For I have given unto them the word which thou gavest me."

2. For the second branch, whatever is not done of faith (that is upon a persuasion that we please God in what we are doing) is sin, (Romans 4:23). Now faith is grounded on the word. And how can a man be persuaded he pleases God in that service he offers to him, unless he has his word for the service he offers? For if we follow our own good intent, while we think we please God, we may most highly offend him. The Jews, when they killed the Apostles, thought they did God good service, John 16:2, and so did Paul when he was exceedingly mad against the

faithful and compelled them to blaspheme, (Acts 26:11). He says that this was then the height of his zeal when he persecuted the Church, (cf. Phil. 3:6).

The first *use* of this doctrine is to teach us, 1. to esteem this a singular prerogative, that the Lord has not suffered us to walk in our own ways, (Acts 14:16), but to be thankful that we have the word, and to make our use of it. This was the chief preferment of the Jew above the Samaritan and all others, (Romans 3:1-2). If any lack this, the god that they serve is not the true god, but an idol, and an imagination of their own, (2 Chron. 15:3). They worship they know not what, where we have a comfortable assurance that the worship we do, pleases God.

2. If therefore you desire to serve and please God, let this be your first care to live under a good ministry, and to get knowledge. Israel was without the true God, while it was without a teaching priest, and without the Law, (2 Chron. 15:3). All the devotion that ignorant people use is but the sacrifice of fools, until they are ready to hear and willing to be instructed that way, (Eccles. 5:1). Therefore, the Lord also complains in Hos. 4:6 that when there is an ignorant priest that cannot instruct them, the people perish for want of knowledge.

3. Count it your wisdom to cleave so precisely to the word, as (in the matters of God's service) not to do anything which you cannot find warranted by the word. Psalm 119:31, "I have cleaved to thy testimonies, O Lord confound me not."

4. Conceive nothing that God has not instructed other than what he has revealed of himself in his word. Now if we apply this to ourselves, we shall find that most

of our people are in no better case then the Samaritans were who worshipped "they knew not what."

1). Indeed, we have the whole word of God, and so they had some of the word. But is our case ever better for that? No, surely it is so much the worse. They lacked it; we have it and condemn it. We count it no prerogative to have it, we make no benefit of it, we do not read it, we do not seek its knowledge, we do not care what ministry we live under, we count it no benefit to live under an able ministry, *etc.* Heb. 2:3, "How shall we escape if we neglect so great salvation?"

2). Though they do join with God's people in his true worship, yet they do not do it on this ground, that they know by the word God will be served in such a way. But the rule they follow is either first the commandment of men, as it is said of the Pharisees, (Matt. 15:9). Or secondly, the custom of the place where they live, as we read the Samaritans of old did, (2 Kings 17:40). Or, thirdly, their own good meaning, contrary to that commandment, "seek not after your own heart," (Num. 15:39).

The second *use* is to justify our religion against the Papists. For it is evident we may truly say to them as our Savior does here, "Ye worship that which ye know not, we worship that which we know." 1. It is not possible they should have any assurance, that they please God in that service they do to him (no matter how confident they seem to be) because they do not worship God according to his word. 2. While they think they worship God, they worship the devil. That is spoken of them certainly in Rev. 9:20, "And the rest of the men which were not killed by these plagues yet repented not of the works of their hands, that they should not worship devils, and idols of gold, and silver, and brass, and stone, and of wood: which neither can see, nor hear, nor walk." For if the Israelites in Aaron's and Jeroboam's time were truly said to *worship devils*, when they worshipped the true God under the similitude of a molten image, then is their worshipping of images no better than idolatry, and worshipping of devils, notwithstanding that they say, that they neither worship the image itself, nor any false god in or by it. The worshipping of the Virgin Mary, as well as the worshipping of Venus, or any of the heathen gods, kneeling before the picture of God the Father, or Christ crucified, as well as kneeling before Baal, is *a worshipping of devils.*

CHAPTER 8:
TRUE IN WORD AND DOCTRINE

To recall, Jesus said, "Ye worship ye know not what: we know what we worship: for salvation is of the Jews," (John 4:22). In this verse three things offer themselves to our consideration. 1. The fault he finds with the Samaritan's worship, "Ye worship that what ye know not what." 2. The commendation he gives to the Jews worship, "we worship that we know." 3. The reason by which he justifies this commendation; he gives to the Jews, "For salvation is of the Jews." It follows now that we proceed to the two last points contained in these words, "We worship that we know, for salvation is of the Jews." In which words, to aid our memory and understanding in them, three things are to be observed. 1. That Christ prophesies of himself that he worshipped God. 2. That he worshipped God as the Jews did. 3. That he affirms salvation is of the Jews.

The first doctrine that we have to learn here is this: that our Savior himself, though he is the Son of God, when he was here on earth, to serve and worship God. 1. He was accustomed diligently to frequent the place of public prayer. Luke 4:16, "He went into the synagogue on the Sabbath day as his custom was." 2. He was accustomed to use prayer in his own family. Luke 9:18, "as he was alone praying, his disciples were with him." 3. He was always accustomed at his meals to give thanks, and pray to God for his blessing on the use of creation, and that (not only when he was to work a miracle, Matt. 14:19, he would look up to heaven and blessed the food that was prepared, that is, gave thanks and prayed) but ordinarily, as in Luke 24:30, "As he sat at table, he took the bread and gave thanks. 4. Besides all these kinds of prayer, he was accustomed to pray in secret, and by himself, Luke 5:16, he kept himself apart, "in the wilderness and prayed." He used this kind of praying in the morning, Mark 1:35, in the morning very early before day he arose, and went out into a solitary place and there prayed. He used it also in the evening. Matt. 14:23, he went up into a mountain alone (having no house of his own, he was accustomed to go abroad into the most solitary place to pray), and when the evening had come, he was there alone. Yes, this was his custom. Luke 22:39, "He went as he was accustomed to the Mount of Olives." 5. He was accustomed to perform this worship of God with gestures and signs of as much reverence, humility and submission, as we shall read any of God's servants have been accustomed to do. Luke 22:41, he "kneeled down and prayed." Matt. 26:39, he fell on his "face and prayed."

The reason why he was diligent in worshipping God in this way was not so much for his own sake, as for us. For he had no need to pray, for he had all creatures in heaven and earth at his command; and by his word was able to do what pleased him. Matt. 8:8-9, "Speak the word only, and ... he shall be healed. For I am a man also in authority," *etc.* Why then did he used to worship God in this way? Surely only for our sake, and not for himself, but in respect of us. There are three reasons for this.

1. That he might purchase to us eternal life. It was necessary he should perfectly keep the law. For in this way the Covenant runs and works. Matt. 19:17, "If thou

wilt enter into life, keep thy commandments, yea perfectly. This is not something fallen men are able to do, therefore he, Gal. 4:4-5, "Was made under the Law that he might redeem them that are under the Law, that we might receive the adoption of sons." Therefore, it was needful for him to fulfill all righteousness, (Matt. 7:5). And this is a chief part of that righteousness God requires of us in his law *that we worship him*, Matt. 22:38, which is the "first and great commandment."

2. That he might give us an example: for that which he speaks of one. Of his actions, it may be said of all that he did in obedience to the moral Law, John 13:15, "I have given you an example that you should do as I have done."

3. That he might obtain for us the Spirit of God, by which we may be made able to do the same. As the disobedience of Adam deserved that all his posterity should lose the image of God, and become like Adam, Romans 5:22 says, "By one man sin entered into the world. So, the active obedience of Christ has deserved that God should renew his image in all the faithful, and give them his quickening Spirit, for, as Romans 8:2 says, "the Law of the spirit of life in Christ Jesus hath made me free from the law of sin and of death."

The use of this doctrine, is to stir every one of us up to a greater conscience and diligence in all the duties of God's worship, especially in prayer. For if the Son of God (that did not have such need to do it in respect of himself) yet used it so constantly, and used it only because the Law requires it of us, and that he might make himself an example to us, and that he might obtain grace for us to do it, then, what excuse can we (that are bound to it by God's Law, and stand in such need of it) have for our ordinary neglect of public prayer, of prayer with our family, of secret and private prayer?

2. The second thing we are to observe here, is this, that our Savior in commending the worship and religion of the Jews, makes himself one of their number, acknowledges himself a member of their church, and professes that he did worship God as they did. From this a doctrine arises for our instruction: that those assemblies that enjoy the word and doctrine of salvation, though they have many corruptions remaining in them are to be acknowledged the true churches of God, and such as none of the faithful may make separation from them. We shall need no further proof of this doctrine then the example of our Savior himself. We can see this if we consider on the one hand how corrupt the state of the Jew's church was in his time, and on the other hand how far forth our Savior communicated with them in the service of God.

1. First, what the state of that church was in his time, we may know if we consider, 1. what the priests and teachers were themselves that had the ordering of God's worship. 2. What the people were, with whom he was to join in God's worship. 3. What the worship itself was, in which he was to communicate.

1. The priests and teachers were ignorant and unlearned, (Matt. 23:16). They were wicked and ungodly, (Matt. 23:3). They had a corrupt and unlawful entrance into their calling, yes, even the high priest himself. For where by God's ordinance he was to hold that office during his life, this office was bought and sold, and made

annually. John 11:49 says, "Caiaphas was high priest for that year."

2. And what were the people? Surely the most of them in all places where he conversed, were notoriously and obstinately wicked. In Nazareth, where he had lived mostly, see what they were. Luke 4:28-29 explains that all that were in the synagogue when they heard this doctrine, were filled with wrath, and rose up and thrust him out of the city, and lead him to the edge of a hill to cast him down headlong. But were they better in other places? No, he upbraided all the cities, where most of his great works were done, "Woe be to thee Chorazin, woe be to thee Bethsaida," (Matt. 11:20-21). And were the people of Jerusalem any better? you shall perceive that by that affection they showed at the passion of our Savior. When Pilate, a Gentile, had made such an offer to them, Luke 23:18 says that all the multitude cried at once, "not him but Barabbas," and in Matt. 27:25, when Pilate had washed his hands and protested for Christ innocence, then answered all the people and said desperately, "his blood be on us and our children."

3. The worship itself that was used in that church had many corruptions in it. 1. They used many superstitious ceremonies, the observation which they urged more strictly then the commandments and ordinances of God, (Mark 7:9). 2. The temple was profaned and made a den of thieves, (Matt. 21:12-13). 3. The discipline and censures of the church were shamefully abused, (John 9:22), for the Jews had decreed that if any confessed that Jesus was the Christ, he should be excommunicated, *ipso facto*. 4. The doctrine was corrupt in many points, as you shall find, (Matt. 5:22-48).

5. Some corruption also was crept into the administration of the sacraments, for they kept it a day after our Savior, (who observed the just time appointed by God) John 19:14, the day of his Passion was but the day of the preparation to the Passover. In this way, we have seen how corrupt the state of the church was. And yet mark how our Savior made no separation from it, but communicated with it in the worship of God. 1. When he was an infant he was circumcised, and by that sacrament incorporated into that church, (Luke 2:21). 2. When his mother was purified, he was brought to the temple and presented to the Lord, and an oblation was given for him, as for other children, (Luke 2:22). 3. He was content to be a hearer of such teachers as taught in that church, (Luke 2:46). 4. He was every Sabbath accustomed to join in public prayer with the congregation that was at Nazareth, (Luke 4:16). 5. He received the sacrament of baptism in a congregation of that people, (Luke 3:21). When all the people were baptized, he was also baptized. 6. He communicated in the Passover with the people, and the priests, (John 2:13). 7. He allowed his disciples to hear those teachers, (Matt. 23:12). Yes, he commanded the leper whom he cleansed, to go and show himself to the Priest, and offer his gift in the temple, (Matt. 8:4).

The reasons why all men are bound to count such assemblies the true churches as enjoy the word and doctrine of salvation, and may not separate from them for their corruptions, are the following:

1. So long as God continues his word and the doctrine of salvation to a people, so long it is evident God dwells among them, and has not forsaken them. "I will set my Tabernacle among you *(by which he meaneth his solemn*

worship, whereof this is a principal part, Lev. 26:11-12) and my
soul shall not abhor you. And I will walk among you, and
I will be your God, and ye shall be my people." "In Judah
God is known, his name is great in Israel, (Psalm 76:12).
"In Salem also is his Tabernacle and his dwelling place in
Sion," (Psalm 76:2). And until God has forsaken a church,
no man may forsake it. For shall we be holier and hate
corruption more than the Lord? It is no sufficient warrant
for any to separate from a Church, because it is guilty of
such sins and corruptions as deserve God *should* forsake it;
and for which God in his word has threatened that he
will forsake it. Until it may appear to us God has indeed
forsaken it, and put in execution that which he has justly
threatened against it, no man may forsake it. Though
adultery (either in the man or the wife) gives just cause of
separation, and that the bond of wedlock should be
broken, so as the innocent party may justly forsake the
offender. Yet, until a bill of divorce has passed between
them, they remain *still* man and wife, notwithstanding
that sin. The woman whom her husband had wronged in
this way, is still called his wife, (Mal. 2:15). Esau had
justly deserved to lose the prerogative of his birthright
and superiority he had over his brother when he had
despised it and sold it, (Gen. 25:34), and also Saul was to
be deprived of his kingdom. God by his decree and oracle
had said of Esau and Jacob, "The elder shall serve the
younger," (Gen. 25:23). And of Saul and David, that he
had rejected the one, and appointed the other to reign in
his stead, (1 Sam. 13:14 and 15:23, 26, 28). And yet until
the Lord saw it was good to put his decree and oracle in
execution, and actually to depose the one from his
birthright, and the other from his kingdom, Jacob

acknowledges Esau his Lord and superior, (Gen. 32:4-5), and so did David think this of Saul, (1 Sam. 24:7-9). So though a church has many corruptions that are in it, and though it might be unworthy of the name of Christ's Church, and also such as the Lord has threatened to make it no church, yet until the Lord has put his threat into execution, and taken away his tabernacle and worship from it; it is still to be acknowledged and reverenced as the Church of Christ.

2. Because no separation may be made from those assemblies where men may be assured to find and attain to salvation. "Lord to whom shall we go, thou hast the words of eternal life," Peter says to our Savior. This accounts a sufficient reason why they might not leave him, (John 6:68). But men may be sure to find and attain to salvation in such assemblies where the ministry of the word, and the doctrine of salvation is continued. For the word and Gospel of Christ is called *salvation* here, and in Heb. 2:3. It is the ordinary means ordained of God to bring men to salvation, (Romans 1:16; 1 Cor. 1:21). Yes, it is at one time or other effectual in all God's elect that enjoy it. James 1:21 calls it the "engrafted word which is able to save your souls."

This is useful to teach us what to judge of our church, and of the Brownists, that separate themselves from it. 1. We may not deny, but that there is just cause of fear, that God may take away his tabernacle from among us, and remove our candlestick. Even the general decay of our first love may cause us to fear it, (Rev. 2:5). And the great neglect of the church censures on scandalous offenders, in respect of what the Apostle says, "know ye not that a little leaven leaveneth the whole lump," (1 Cor.

5:6). But specially the general increase of all filthy and abominable sins in the land, "thy camp shall be holy, that he see no unclean thing in thee, and turn away from thee," (Deut. 32:14). "Seest thou not (the Lord says in Ezek. 8:6), the great abominations that the house of Israel committeth here, that I should go far off from my sanctuary?" 2. Though we acknowledge our church to be a true church, yet may we not communicate with it in any corruptions, that shall be detected or approved to be in it. In this we have our Savior's example to guide us. Though he esteemed the church of the Jews to be a true Church, and joined with it in God's worship, yet would he not communicate with it in the least corruption. He would not use so much as their superstitious purifications, (Mark 7:6-7). When they put off the Passover a day longer then God had appointed, he would not join with them in that, (Matt. 26:17). 3. We should mourn for, and show our dislike to, those things that are evil in our church, so did the faithful before the captivity, (Ezek. 9:4). So did Christ, (Luke 19:41). But we may not separate ourselves, nor deny it to be a true Church for the reasons above alleged.

2. To convince the Papists of error, in their doctrine concerning the notes of the true church. None of their notes are proper and infallible; for the profession and preaching of the true doctrine in all fundamental points is the only proper and certain note of the true church, as we see here in the argument Christ uses to prove the church and worship of the Jews to be the true worship and church of God. For "salvation is of the Jews." This was the chief privilege, the chief badge and cognizance of the old church, that the oracles of God

were committed to them. They enjoyed the true doctrine of salvation, (Psalm 147:19-20; Romans 3:2). And in this way the Apostle describes the true church under the Gospel. He calls it the household of God "built upon the foundation of the Apostles and Prophets, Jesus Christ himself, being the chief Corner-stone," (Eph. 2:19-20). He calls it also "the pillar and ground of truth," (1 Tim. 3:25).

CHAPTER 9:
Spirit and Truth

"But the hour cometh, and now is, when the true worshippers shall worship the Father in spirit and in truth: for the Father seeketh such to worship him. God is a Spirit: and they that worship him must worship him in spirit and in truth," (John 4:23-24).

We have already considered the answer our Savior makes to the question which the woman of Samaria moved him to answer, consisting of two parts. 1. A commendation of that outward worship the Jews used in comparison of that of the Samaritans. 2. A discommendation of that outward worship of God which the Jews used in comparison of that which God would shortly establish in his church. The former part of this answer is set down in the 22nd verse, which we have finished. The latter part of his answer is contained in these words which we began with. The sum and effect of this part of his answer is this: that though the worship which the Jews then offered to God was far better than that of the Samaritans, yet this ceremonial worship which the Jews used (though it were commanded of God himself) was not so much to be esteemed as she thought, but should shortly be abolished. Instead of this, another form of God's worship should be established, which should not consist in ceremonies and shadows which suited at best man's carnal and corrupt nature. It should now become spiritual as best agreeing to the nature of

God, and have in it the truth and substance of all that which was figured and shadowed in those ceremonies.

There are two parts to this text. 1. A proposition or doctrine concerning the true worship that Christians are to give to God. True worshippers shall worship the Father in spirit and in truth; which is repeated with some increase, they that worship him, *must worship* him in spirit and in truth. 2. The reasons of this doctrine and proposition are also two. 1. Because the Father even seeks or desires to have such worshippers. 2. Because God is a spirit, and must therefore have such worship and service done to him as is suitable to his nature.

The proposition or doctrine is enlarged, or set forth by two circumstances. 1. The person to whom this spiritual worship is to be given, which is the Father. 2. The time when this spiritual worship shall be given to him, "the hour commeth, and now is."

First, then it is here to be observed: that our Savior speaks of the worship that Christians should give to God (which should be far better than that which the Jews then used). It calls on God to whom this worship was to be offered, who is designated as the Father, and that so often, even three times, once in verse 21 and twice in this verse. What is the reason for this repetition? Surely our Savior by this intimates one chief cause why the Christians under the Gospel should offer God better service then the Jews had done under the Law, because they shall conceive of God as their Father. It is true, the Lord was a Father to his people under the Law, and so they thought of him in this way. But the Lord has revealed his fatherly affection and love in Christ more fully and clearly to us, then he had done to his church under the Law. Gal. 4:3-5, "We, when we were children, were in bondage under the elements of the world; But when the fullness of the time was come, God sent forth his Son made of a woman made under the Law, To redeem them that were under the Law, that we might receive the adoption of sons."

From this we have this doctrine to learn: that no man can worship God rightly until he knows God to be his Father. The better a man is persuaded and assured of God's fatherly love to him in Christ, the better service he shall give to him. Therefore, our Savior teaching us to pray, bids us say, "Our Father," (Matt. 6:9), as if he should say, "do not presume to ask any petition of God, until you can so conceive, and be persuaded of him as Father." And the Apostle tells us it is the Spirit of adoption that makes us able to pray, and makes this the voice of the spirit of prayer. It cries, "Abba, Father," (Romans 8:15). Yes, he makes it an impossible thing for any man to pray aright without this assurance. Romans 10:14 says, "How shall they call on him in whom they have not believed?"

The reason of it is first, because until we know God is our Father, and loves us in Christ, we cannot be assured that he will accept us. When we know he is our Father in Christ, it makes us go to him with boldness and confidence. In Christ we have boldness and access with confidence through faith in him, (Eph. 3:12). "I will arise and go to my father (the prodigal says in Luke 15:18) and will say unto him, father I have sinned against heaven and before thee." Though he had sinned so outrageously, yet the consideration that it was his father he was to go to gave him boldness. It gives us assurance, that notwithstanding our infirmities he will accept us. "I will spare him (and deal gently and indulgently with him the Lord says, Mal. 3:17) as a man spareth his son that serveth him." When the prodigal was yet a great way off, his father saw him, and had compassion, and ran, and fell on his neck, and kissed him, (Luke 15:20). And nothing graces our prayers more with God then this confidence and boldness, "Let us come boldly to the throne of grace, that we may obtain mercy, and find grace to help in time of need," the Apostle says, (Heb. 4:16). But without this faith and persuasion that God is our Father, we can have no assurance that any thing we do in his service pleases him. Without faith it is impossible to please God, (Heb. 11:6). And the best things we do in his service without this assurance that we please him in doing such service *is sin*, as Romans 14:23 says, "Whatsoever is not of faith is sin."

Secondly, because until a man is persuaded of God's love and fatherly affection towards him in Christ, he can never serve him in love, nor with a good heart, but on some by-respects, on a servile fear, or hope of merit, (Heb. 10:22). We can never draw near to God with a true heart, until we have assurance of faith, and our hearts are sprinkled from an evil conscience. No man can truly love God until he is persuaded by the Spirit of God's love to him. "We love God, because he loved us first," (1 John 4:19). True love comes from a pure heart, and a good conscience, and faith unfeigned, (1 Tim. 1:5). And whatsoever service we do to God, unless it proceeds out of a good heart, and from love to God, it cannot please him. Though a man should give his body to be burned in martyrdom, yet if that does not proceed from his love to God, it would profit him nothing, (1 Corinthians 13:3).

For what man would accept of any service from him that he knows does not love him?

The *use* of the doctrine is to exhort us to get good assurance to our hearts that God is our Father, that he bears a fatherly affection to us. Above all sins strive against infidelity. "Examine yourselves whither ye be in the faith, prove yourselves," (2 Cor. 13:5). Many lack this assurance, and do not seek it; many seem to have it, and do not have it. I will give you four notes to try it by.

1. God is a Father to no man, but in and through Christ. John 1:12, "So many as received him, to them gave he power to become the sons of God, even to them that believe in his name." Galatians 4:5, "He hath redeemed us that were under the Law, that we might receive the adoption of sons." A man must ground his assurance and confidence that God is his Father only on Christ. If he grounds it on the idea that God has made him, and preserved him, *etc.*, his assurance is in vain.

2. He that is persuaded indeed, that God is his Father, will boldly resort to him in prayer. "Because ye are sons, God hath sent forth the spirit of his Son into your hearts, crying Abba Father," (Gal. 4:6). They that seldom pray, or pray with no willingness and cheerfulness, or pray with no confidence, without a doubt are not persuaded that God is their Father.

3. He that is persuaded that God is his Father, will not murmur against, nor be put out of heart by any of God's corrections, but be persuaded of his love even in affliction, according to that of the Apostle, Heb. 12:7-9, "If ye endure chastening, God dealeth with you as with sons: for what son is he whom the father chasteneth not?" And Romans 15:3, "Being justified by faith we glory even in

tribulation." They that in the time of their peace and prosperity only are confident in God's love, but have no heart, no comfort in affliction, are not indeed persuaded that God is their Father.

4. He that is indeed persuaded that the Lord bears the affection of a Father to him, will bear the affection of a child to God; will love him, and be careful to please him, fearful to offend him. Mal. 1:6, "If I be your Father where is mine honor?" As Heb. 10:22 instructs, there is no drawing near to God in assurance of faith, until we are sprinkled in our hearts from an evil conscience, and washed in our bodies also. They that have no care to please God, nor fear to offend him, without a doubt are not persuaded that God is their Father.

Now come we to the principal doctrine which our Savior teaches us in this place, namely, that the only true worship of God, the only worship that pleases God (now especially under the Gospel) is that which is spiritual. The worship that is proper to the Gospel, true Christian worship, is spiritual. This is what our Savior says here, "The hour commeth, and now it is, that the true worshippers shall worship the Father in spirit, and in truth." And again, "They that worship him, must worship him" in this way.

Now for the right understanding of this doctrine, six questions must be moved and resolved.

1. What our Savior means here, by worshipping God in spirit. The answer is, that to worship God in spirit, is to worship him without such ceremonies as were under the Law. This appears by this note of diversity which our Savior here uses. "But," as if he should say, the worship the Jews now use (which chiefly consists in their

sacrifices, oblations, purifications, and such like ceremonies) is good, because it is done on the knowledge of God's will revealed in his word. *But* now such as worship God rightly, shall worship him in another manner. Namely, not in such ceremonies, but in spirit, and truth. So, that to worship God in spirit, is opposed to the ceremonial worship, because that was not a spiritual, but a carnal worship. See this in that opposition Paul makes in Gal. 3:3, "Are ye so foolish? having begun in the spirit, are ye now made perfect by the flesh?" So, the ceremonial Law is called a carnal commandment, (Heb. 7:16), and all the ceremonies are called carnal rites, (Heb. 9:10). This is a strange term to be given to the worship that God himself ordained. But the ceremonies are called this because, 1. They were all outward, and bodily actions. Yes, if we look over all the ceremonial Law, we shall find nothing enjoined either to the priests, or people, but external and bodily things. The service of the spirit and conscience, is seldom or never mentioned. Heb. 9:9-10, "The first Tabernacle was a figure for the time then present; in which were offered both gifts, and sacrifices, that could not make him that did the service perfect, as pertaining to the conscience, which stood only in meats, and drinks, and divers washings, and carnal ordinances imposed on them, until the time of reformation." Where, the service God required under the Gospel is in a manner wholly inward, and spiritual. For in this way the Lord speaks of the days of the Gospel in which he will make a New Covenant with his people, Jer. 31:34, "They shall all know me from the least of them, to the greatest of them, saith the Lord." And verse 33, "I will put my Law in their inward parts, and write it in their hearts." Now the Lord still calls for the service of the spirit, and heart at our hands. Our preaching does not please God unless it is the action of our spirit. Paul served God with his spirit in the Gospel of his Son, (Romans 1:9). Our hearing does not please him unless it is the action of our heart and spirit. The Holy Spirit opened the heart of Lydia to attend this preaching by Paul, (Acts 16:14). Our prayers do not please God unless they are the service of the heart and spirit. "Pray with all prayer and supplication in the spirit," (Eph. 6:18). Our singing is the same, "making melody in your hearts to the Lord," (Eph. 5:19). Our communicating in the sacrament does not please God unless it is the service of our spirit. No man receives worthily unless he examines himself before, and is able to discern the body of the Lord in that ordinance, (1 Corinthians 11:29).

2. They are called *carnal* because they were all transitory and were to endure but for a time. To this reason the Apostle has respect, Heb. 7:16, 18, when he calls the Law of the Levitical Priesthood a carnal commandment, because it was to be disannulled. Where, our worship shall continue, and never be altered, and in this respect the Apostle prefers the state of the church now, before that of the Old Testament, (Heb. 1:1-2), that where the Lord delivered his will to his church not all at once, but at various times by the prophets, he has by his Son fully made his mind known to us in these last days; not at sundry times, but at once. And therefore, also, the Apostle Jude calls it "the faith that was once (for all) delivered unto the saints," (Jude 1:3). In this respect the whole time since Christ's ascension is called also the end of the world, (1 Cor. 10:11) and the last times, (2 Tim. 3:1; Acts 2:17; 1 Peter 1:20; 1 John 2:18).

3. Because their effect and fruit reaches no further than to the body, and outward man, they could not make holy concerning the conscience, the one that offered the service, (Heb. 9:9 and 10:1). They could not make those who came to serve to it perfect, but sanctified only as concerning the purifying of the flesh, (Heb. 9:13). Therefore, they are called, Gal. 4:9, "weak and beggarly elements." Where the service of God under the Gospel, works wholly (in a manner) on the conscience, and inward man. The Kingdom of God (the true religion and its sincere profession) is not in word, but in power, (1 Cor. 4:20). If the word is preached, and heard, the sacraments administered, and received, prayer used as they ought, they will work on the conscience, not only on the outward man. Therefore, it is called in 2 Cor. 3:8, "the ministration of the Spirit."

4. It is called a carnal worship, because it is very pleasing to the natural, and carnal man. He makes great conscience of it, and delights much in it. In which respect also the Apostle says, Gal. 4:3, it was a service fit for God's people when they were children. Our Savior observes the Pharisees to have been very precise in the observation of the ceremonial Law, and to have made much more conscience of it then of the moral. They paid a tithe of mint, and anise, and cumin, and omitted the weightier matters of the Law, judgment, mercy, and fidelity, (Matt. 23:23). And the Lord by his prophet speaking of such, as for their wickedness, he calls the princes of Sodom and people of Gomorrah, saying they offered a multitude of Sacrifices, brought many oblations to God and much incense, observed diligently the new moons, and Sabbaths, and solemn days, (Isaiah 1:11, 13).

Yes, all heathen men and pagans have had their sacrifices and ceremonies. Balaam and Balaak used them, (Num. 23:1-4). Where the service that God requires of us under the Gospel, is such as no natural man can relish, or find any savor in. No, none but such as have the Spirit can make any account of our worship, can hear, receive and pray with their conscience and with delight. 1 John 4:6, "He that is of God, heareth us, he that is not of God, heareth us not." So, 1 Cor. 2:14, "The natural man receiveth not the things of the Spirit of God, for they are foolishness unto him, neither can he know them, because they are spiritually discerned." So, we see what our Savior here means by worshipping God in spirit.

CHAPTER 10:
WORSHIP IN TRUTH

What does the Savior mean when he says that we must worship in truth? The answer is, to worship God in truth, is to worship him without such ceremonies, as were under the Law. This appears by that note of diversity here used (*but*) which I observed before. Truth, then, is not here opposed either to a false worship, or to hypocrisy, but to *ceremonial worship*. So that in both of these words mean one and the same thing, is understood by our Savior. And it is as if he should have said, "the true worshippers now shall worship God without ceremonies." Yet are neither of these words superfluous, but as *spirit* is opposed to the ceremonial worship, as it was an external, and carnal worship, so *truth* is opposed to it since it was full of shadows, and figures. And in this way is this word *truth* taken. Dan. 7:16, "I asked him the truth of (that is the meaning, and that that was signified by) all this, so he told me, and made me the interpretation of the things." All the ceremonies were shadows, (Col. 2:7). The whole Tabernacle was a figure, (Heb. 9:9). Yes, as Heb. 10:1 explains, the Law had the shadow of good things to come, and not the very live picture of them.

Now our Savior says that the truth and substance of those things that were shadowed by the ceremonial worship, shall be in our worship under the Gospel. We shall find that the ceremonies were shadows, and figures, not only of Christ, and of those good things we receive by him, but also of those graces, and good things as should be in the faithful members of Christ.

1. Circumcision was but a shadow. What was the truth, and substance of it? Surely the circumcising and cutting off (by true mortification) the corruption of the heart, (Romans 2:28). That is not circumcision which is outward. This is as if he should say, "that was but a shadow." Then, verse 29, circumcision is that of the heart in the spirit, and not in the letter. The Jew had but the shadow of circumcision, every true worshipper now has the truth, and its substance.

2. The casting of leaven out of all their houses in the feast of the Passover, Exod. 12:15, was but a shadow. What was its truth and substance? That they that would serve God with comfort, and joy must purge out the old leaven of maliciousness, and wickedness, and keep this feast with the unleavened bread of sincerity and truth, (1 Cor. 5:7-8). The Jew had but the shadow of the Passover, but every true worshipper now has its substance.

3. The Jews had in their worship many propitiatory sacrifices for obtaining of the remission of all kind of sins that they had committed against God, (Heb. 9:22). Without shedding of blood there was no remission. And the Law was, that whosoever brought one of these sacrifices to God, must (in presenting it to be offered by the priest) put his hand on its head, and lean on it, or else it could not be accepted of the Lord for his atonement, (Lev. 1:4). And that when it was slain by the priest, its blood must be sprinkled on the people, (Exod. 24:8). Now this was but a figure and a shadow. What was its truth and substance? Surely, that no man ever shall have Christ's sacrifice accepted by God for his atonement, unless by a lively faith he can apply Christ to himself, leaning and relying with confidence of heart on him.

Unless he is able to say, "this is my sacrifice, this is he that has born my sins and my punishment," as Gal. 2:20 teaches. "He has loved me, and given himself for me." And Isaiah 53:4, "Surely he hath born our infirmities, and carried our sorrows." The blood of Christ will do a man no good, unless it is sprinkled and applied to his own conscience by the Spirit of God, (1 Peter 1:2). The elect are to be saved through the obedience and sprinkling of the blood of Christ, which is therefore called "the blood of sprinkling," which speaks better things than the blood of Abel, (Heb. 12:24).

4. They also had many eucharistical sacrifices, *sacrifices of thanksgiving*, which were called peace-offerings. When they would solemnly profess their thankfulness to God for any blessing received, they were accustomed to do it by sacrifices and peace-offerings. Yes, as the cause of their thanksgiving exceeded this, so were they accustomed to exceed and abound in these sacrifices. So, it is said of the people of God after their return to Jerusalem out of their captivity, Neh. 12:53, "The same day they offered great sacrifices, and rejoiced, for God had given them great joy." And of Solomon it is said, that at the dedication of the temple, he offered a sacrifice of "two and twenty thousand bullocks: and a hundreth and twenty thousand sheep," (2 Chron. 7:5). Now this manner of serving God was *a figure and shadow*. What was the truth and substance of it? Surely the spiritual sacrifices by which Christians are to praise God, and show themselves thankful to him for his mercies, were figured and shadowed by those sacrifices, as *namely:*

1. A contrite heart. When a man (out of the consideration of God's mercy) can unfeignedly repent and

lament, that he has by his sins offended so good a Father, this is a true sacrifice of thanksgiving, for as Psalm 51:17 says, "the sacrifices of God are a broken spirit."

2. Obedience. When a man can (in thankfulness to God for his mercies) sacrifice himself to God, resign himself wholly to his obedience and service, this is a true sacrifice of thanksgiving, Romans 11:1-2, "I beseech you by the mercies of God that you give up your bodies a living sacrifice, holy, acceptable to God, which is your reasonable serving of God; and fashion not yourselves like unto this world, but be you changed by the renewing of your mind."

3. Prayer. When a man can find, that the experience he has had of God's goodness, stirs him up to go often to God in prayer, and so to depend on him for all good things, this is a true sacrifice of thanksgiving. Heb. 13:15, let us therefore by him "offer the sacrifice of praise always to God," that is the fruit of the lips which confess his name. And Psalm 116, when David had said, verse 12, "What shall I render to the Lord for all his benefits towards me?" He resolves himself in verse 13, "I will take the cup of salvation, and call upon the name of the Lord." And Psalm 50, when the Lord had showed to the Jews how small a pleasure he took in all their sacrifices, he sets down, in verses 14-15, what the true sacrifices of thanksgiving are which he delighted in: offer to God praise, and pay your vows to the most high, and call on him in the day of trouble.

4. Good works. When a man in thankfulness and love to God (for all his mercies) deals justly and mercifully with all men for the Lord's sake, then he offers to God a true sacrifice of thanksgiving, (Heb. 13:16), to do

good, and to distribute. Do not forget that with such sacrifices God is well pleased. So, Paul calls the relief which the Philippians sent him when he was in prison at Rome, an odor that smelled sweet, a sacrifice acceptable and pleasant to God, (Phil. 4:18). So then we see now what our Savior means when he says, the true worshippers shall worship God *in truth*. The sacraments and sacrifices of the Jews were but shadows and figures. True worshippers of God under the Gospel shall have in them the truth and substance of that which was shadowed in those ceremonies. The true and substantial worship of God consists in a lively faith, unfeigned repentance, absolute obedience to the will of God in all things, hearty prayer, love, justice, mercifulness, sincerity, and other such graces of God's Spirit.

In this way I have gone through the two first questions in order to better understand this doctrine. In the other four that follow, I will be a bit more brief.

The third question is, what does our Savior mean by the "hour that commeth and now is?" When should the true worshippers worship God in Spirit and in truth? When should this spiritual and substantial worship of God that we have heard of, begin? Was the ceremonial worship at an end when he spoke this?

I answer *no*, for after this time, (Matt. 8:4), Christ sends the leper to the priest, and bids him to offer his gift appointed in the ceremonial Law. And Christ himself observed the feast of unleavened bread, at which time the text says, Luke 22:7, "the Passover must be killed." This hour and time did not begin until Christ had suffered, and was glorified, and ascended into heaven. This is presently when Christ had said in his Passion, John 19:30, "It is finished." It is said, Matt. 27:51, the vail of the temple was rent "in twain from the top to the bottom." This was the time the ceremonial worship abrogated. And when Christ ascended and was glorified, then began the time when the true worshippers should worship God in spirit and in truth. This is plain, John 7:39, "This spake he of the Spirit, which they that believed in him, should receive, for the Holy Ghost was not yet come, because that Jesus was not yet glorified." Now because this time of Christ's Passion and Ascension was at hand even now, therefore our Savior says here, the "hour commeth, and now is."

The fourth question is, was not God worshipped in spirit and truth before the time of Christ's Passion and Ascension? Did all God's people under the Law, and such as lived in Christ's time, Simeon, Anna, Mary, Zachariah, and Elizabeth worship God only in ceremony, and shadow, not in spirit and truth?

I answer. 1. That even under the Law, the Lord was never satisfied with a ceremonial worship, but did ever require to be worshipped in spirit and truth. So this is what Samuel said to Saul, 1 Sam. 15:22, "Hath the Lord as great pleasure in burnt offerings, and sacrifices, as when the voice of the Lord is obeyed? To obey is better then sacrifice, and to hearken is better then the fat of rams." So Psalm 51:16, "Thou desirest no sacrifice, though I would give it, thou delightest not in burnt offerings." And Hos. 6:6, "I desired mercy, and not sacrifice, and the knowledge of God more then burnt offerings." And Micah 6:8, "He hath showed the O man what is good; and what doth the Lord require of thee, but to do justly, and to love mercy, and to walk humbly with thy God." Mark. 12:33 says to love the Lord "with all thy heart, and with all thy understanding, and with all thy soul, and with all thy strength," and to love a man's neighbor as himself is more then all burnt offerings and sacrifices. 2. The people of God under the Law did not worship him only in ceremony, but in spirit and truth. So David, when he had said in Psalm 40:6, "Sacrifice and offering thou dost not desire," he adds verse 8, "I desired to do thy will O my God, yea thy Law is within my heart." And the ministry they enjoyed, was not only the ministry of the letter, but of the Spirit as well. So it is said of the ministry of Levi, Malachi 2:6, he did "turn many away from iniquity."

But though this is true, yet our Savior says here, "The hour commeth, and now is," as if he should have said, it has *not been so before*, because, 1. Though God gave his Spirit to his people then, yet, not so generally then as now. But then only to the Jews, now, as Acts 2:17 shows, "In the latter days I will pour out of my Spirit upon all flesh." Not so fully to them before, in comparison to those that received it as now. The prophet speaking of the days of Christ says in Isaiah 11:9, "The earth shall be full of the knowledge of God as the waters that cover the sea." And, Zech. 12:8, "He that is feeble among them in that day shall be as David." 2. Though the Lord also required then a spiritual worship, and the faithful performed it, yet they did not serve God only in spirit and in truth, but also in ceremonies and shadows, as God so required them to do, (Lev. 4:3). Yes, he required it of them with stipulations and a great penalty, Exod. 5:3, "Let us go and sacrifice unto the Lord, lest he fall upon us with pestilence, or with the sword." Yes, God was pleased and delighted in it greatly. It is therefore called an oblation made by fire "for a sweet savor to the Lord," (Lev. 1:9). So that these words are to be understood comparatively, as if he should say, "Though the Father were worshipped in spirit and truth before, yet in comparison of that, he shall be, after my death and ascension, not worshipped in spirit and truth as before." So is that place also to be understood, Heb. 9:8, "The way into the holiest of all (into heaven) was not yet opened while the first Tabernacle was standing." That is not so wide, not made so common, not so fully opened as afterward.

From here arises the fifth question. Must we now under the Gospel serve God only in spirit? Does God now require of us no other worship but that only that is spiritual?

I answer: 1. That God has appointed for us a bodily and outward worship as well. Yes, he has given us some significant ceremonies to use in his worship and service. Namely, both of our sacraments are visible signs of invisible grace. He requires not only the service of our hearts, but also the service of our tongue and knees in calling on his name, and singing of Psalms; the service of our ears in hearkening to his word; the service of our eyes in beholding that that is done in the administration of the sacraments; the service of our whole body in presenting ourselves before him in the public assemblies. So that it is but the speech of a profane hypocrite to say in this way "though I do not make that show as others do, though I usually do not to kneel and say my prayers either with my family, or apart, though I do not go so much to church as others do, yet I serve God as well as they do because I serve him in my heart. I lift up my heart to him. I serve him in my calling. I get my living by my earnest labor. I deal justly with all men. And since God is a Spirit, and will be worshipped in spirit, it is the service of the heart that he looks for, he does not care for these hypocritical shows. It does not matter if I serve him outwardly, so long as I have a good heart."

And there are three *reasons*, why men may not be content in themselves to serve God only in spirit, but must serve him outwardly and bodily as well.

1. In respect of God: for he having created, redeemed, and sanctified our bodies as well as our souls, is of right to have homage and service done him by both, 1 Cor. 6:19-20, "Ye are not your own, for ye are bought with a price: therefore glorify God in your body, and in your spirit, for they are God's."

2. In respect of ourselves, for the service we do to God in our bodies, is a great and necessary help to our spirits, Romans 10:17, "Faith commeth by hearing."

3. In respect of others: for our light should so shine before men, that they may see our good works (see that we worship and serve God) and glorify our Father which is in heaven, (Matt. 5:6).

Why then (may you say) how does God's service now differ from that which was under the law, seeing the faithful then served him in spirit and truth as well as we must now? And we serve God with an outward ceremonial worship as well as they did?

I answer, the difference stands in these two points. 1. Though we have some outward worship, and significant ceremonies now, yet we have nothing so much in our outward worship which is required of us, as was of them; nor so many significant ceremonies as they had. Besides their sabbaths and new moons, they had many other festival days which they were bound to observe;

their temple and everything in it, their sacrifices, their offerings, and purifications, their priests, and everything that belonged to them, were significant ceremonies. We have but a little outward worship in comparison required, and but two only significant ceremonies left to us by Christ. 2. Even that outward worship that we have is much more plain and spiritual then theirs was, much more effectual to work on the understanding and conscience then theirs were. Our ceremonies much more clearly set forth and represent that which they signify then their ceremonies did.

Did not circumcision more clearly represent the remission of our sins, and regeneration by the merits of Christ's blood, then baptism? Did not slaying and eating of the paschal lamb more clearly represent the Passion of Christ, and the nourishment our souls receive by it, then the Lord's Supper does?

I answer no. For they represented Christ that was to come, and take our nature on him, and perform in this the work of our redemption. Ours represent Christ that has come, and has already taken our nature on him, and performed fully the work of our redemption. And therefore, theirs were both bloody sacraments, to show and figure to God's people that blood was to be shed for obtaining these good things for them. Ours are without blood, to show to us, that Christ's blood is already shed for us, and that there is no more blood to be shed for our sins. Therefore, Christ instituting the Lord's Supper, calls the wine his "blood that was already shed," (Matt. 26:28). So that as the faithful that lived in Christ's time, and saw all that which was performed which God had promised concerning him, were much more confirmed in their faith, and had much more comfort in the knowledge of Christ then those that had that lived before, and believed in him. "Your father Abraham rejoiced to see my day, and he saw it (by faith) and was glad," (John 8:58). "I tell you that many prophets and kings have desired to see those things which ye see, and have not seen them, and to hear those things which ye hear, and have not heard them, (Luke 10:24). When Simeon (who had waited for the Consolation of Israel, that is, for Christ's coming, (Luke 2:25) had both seen Christ and taken him up in his arms, he was so comforted that he desired to live no longer but cried, "Lord now lettest thou thy servant depart in peace, according to thy word, for mine eyes have seen thy salvation," (Luke 2:28-30). So, our sacraments that represent Christ as one that has already come, and has performed the work of our redemption, must necessarily make much more for the confirmation of our faith, and comfort of our conscience, then theirs did.

The sixth question follows. What was the cause of this alteration in the worship of God, that the Lord (in whom there is no variableness nor shadow of change, James 1:17) would be served after one manner under the Law, and another under the Gospel? Under the Law with many ceremonies, under the Gospel in a more spiritual manner?

I answer, that this did not grow from any alteration in the Lord, but from the change that was in the state and condition of his Church. In appointing ceremonies and pompous worship under the law, the Lord did not respect so much his own disposition, as the weaknesses of that people, and condition of those times.

1. The Lord gave them that kind of worship to restrain them from idolatry, which otherwise he saw they were strongly inclined to. Now that the church is of greater strength, he has appointed another manner of worship more agreeable to his own nature, and disposition.

2. That worship was fittest for the church in her child-hood. The outward worship is easily performed, though it had many straight conditions annexed to it, as we may see by that question and offer that hypocrites made. Micah 6:6-7, "Shall I come before him with burnt offerings, with calves of a year old? Will the Lord be pleased with thousands of rams, or with ten thousands of rivers of oil? Shall I give my first-born for my transgression, the fruit of my body for the sin of my soul?" Inward and spiritual worship is not only hard, but impossible to be performed without the grace of God.

And therefore, it pleased God in tender regard to the weaknesses of his church under the Law, to appoint to them more of that outward worship, and to accept of their spiritual service though it were in small measure. But, now he requires a greater measure of spiritual worship, and enjoins little of the other. With children we require a bodily service, in saying their prayers, and graces, and catechism. And though they have little or no understanding and sense of that they say, yet we take it in good part.

3. Though God was able to have established his spiritual worship before, and to have given his Spirit to his church under the Law in as great measure as now, yet was it fit that this honor should be reserved to the coming of Christ in the flesh. He being the Son of righteousness,

it was fitting that at his rising all those mists and shadows should vanish away.

It was fitting that God should honor and solemnize the marriage of his Son with his church, and his triumph over Satan, *etc.,* by bestowing his gifts and graces more abundantly on men, then he had done before. To this the Apostle has respect when he says in Ephesians 4:8, "When he ascended up on high, he lead captivity captive, and gave gifts to men."

CHAPTER 11:
THE FATHER AND TRUE WORSHIP

We have seen that John 4:23-24 consist of a doctrine, and of two reasons that are used to confirm it. The *doctrine* is this, that they only worship God aright (specially now under the Gospel) when they worship him not with a ceremonious worship, but in spirit and truth. We concluded that doctrine in the last chapter, and it remains now that we proceed to the *reasons* that our Savior gives here to prove that they that would now worship God with a ceremonious worship (as the Jews had done then) do not worship him rightly, but only those who worship him in spirit and in truth worship him rightly.

The reason is in these words, "for the Father requireth even such to worship him," or the "Father even seeketh and desireth such worshippers." The force of this reason stands in three points.

1. That worship only is to be given to God (not which pleases and seems best to us) but which he requires, and delights in. It is no better then idolatry, and spiritual whoredom for us to follow our own heart and good meaning in this case, (Num. 15:39).[18] Yes, a man shall highly provoke God if he offers him any service that he does not require. Nadab and Abihu were destroyed with fire from heaven for offering incense with fire that he had

---

[18] "And it shall be unto you for a fringe, that ye may look upon it, and remember all the commandments of the LORD, and do them; and that ye seek not after your own heart and your own eyes, after which ye use to go a whoring," (Num. 15:39).

not commanded them to use, (Lev. 10:3). Yes, the care of a Christian must be not only to offer God that service that he requires, but to do it also in that manner as he may please God in doing it, or else he loses his labor. David was exceedingly careful of this in all his prayers. Psalm 19:14, "Let the words of my mouth, and the meditation of my heart, be acceptable in thy sight." And he professes that if God, when he prayed, did not answer him (that is, give him some comfortable assurance that he accepted, and took his prayer in good part) it would be even a death to him. Psalm 28:1, "Be not deaf to me, lest if thou answer me not, I be like to them that go down to the pit." And this should be every Christian's care. Heb. 12:28, "Let us have grace to serve him," so as we may please him.

2. The Lord seeks, and desires to have such to serve him, as worship him in spirit and in truth. He even seeks such worshippers, yes, he is greatly delighted with such worship. It is a strange thing that God should seek or desire this at our hands that we should worship him. For he has no need of our service, neither can he receive any benefit at all by any worship we do to him. If we pray constantly in secret, and constantly frequent the public assemblies, the benefit is wholly our own. Prov. 9:12, "If thou be wise, thou shalt be wise for thy self." What shall the Lord gain by it? Job 37:5, "If thou be righteous, what givest thou to him, or what receiveth he at thy hand?" No, the best service we can do, is so weak and poorly done, as it is a wonder that God does not abhor it. Isaiah 64:6, "All our righteousness is as filthy rags." The best of God's servants seldom please themselves in any service they do to him, but see the cause of shame in the very best actions, and services they have done to him. Neh. 13:2,

"Pardon me O my God according to thy great mercy." Why? What had he done that he craves pardon for? Surely, he had done an excellent piece of service to God; he had showed a marvelous zeal for sanctifying the Sabbath. But, he knew that his good service was so imperfect, so full of stains that he had need of pardon. And yet such is the wonderful goodness of God to those whom he loves in Christ. Such is the delight that he takes in his own graces, in the fruits of his own spirit, that (as if he should receive some great benefit by it) he seeks to us, and desires us to serve him. "Call upon me in the day of trouble," (Psalm 50:15). Seek, ask, knock, that is, pray earnestly and importunately, (Matt. 7:7). Pray without ceasing, (1 Thess. 5:17). You he professes that he takes a marvelous delight in our poor services we offer to him. This is plainly proved by that speech the Lord uses to his church, which is the company of all the faithful. Song of Songs 2:14, "My dove that art in the holes of the rock in the secret places of the stairs, (that is, whose state is most stable and sure, and against whom the gates of hell shall never be able to prevail) show me thy sight (let me see you often, come often to me) let me hear thy voice (pray often to me)." And mark the reason why he tells his church to do this, "For thy voice is sweet, and thy sight comely," (as if he should say, however you think of yourself, whatsoever you judge of your own prayers, I assure you, that in my ear there is no music to that, in my eye there is no person in the world so well favored as you are). This is like the affection that is in us as parents towards our little children when they begin to speak. This makes us delight to hear them prattle, (though to another that prattling does not have that affection and it is very troublesome). And though in another's eye they seem hard favored, yet this fatherly affection makes us to consider them to be very pretty and well favored children. So, this is how it is with the Lord our God. The Fatherly affection he bears to us in Christ, makes him desirous to have us come often to him, to pray and worship him often, and to delight so much in our poor prayers, though in themselves they are not worthy to be delighted in. The Father seeks such worshippers, for in Rev. 5:8 the hearts of all the faithful are compared to golden vials full of odors. What were those odors? The prayers of the saints, of these true worshippers that worship in spirit and truth. Why are the prayers of the godly called *odors*? 1. In respect of the godly themselves, because for the most part they yield a sweet savor, and unspeakable comfort to their own hearts. John 16:24, "Ask that your joy may be full." But: 2. chiefly in respect of the Lord (for the faithful themselves sometimes feel no sweetness in their prayers) but to the Lord their prayers are even as the sweetest odors. Even such prayers as they feel a small sweetness, or delight in, are most pleasant and delightsome to the Lord. Hezekiah felt a small sweetness in that prayer he made, when in his sickness he turned his face to the wall, and wept sorely. This was when his heart was so oppressed with grief that he could not speak, but in his prayer chattered like a swallow, and mourned like a dove, (Isaiah 38:14). But the Lord took great complacency and delight in it, as may appear by the reward he gave him for it presently. For, before the prophet Isaiah (whose message from the Lord you know had been the occasion of that good king's heaviness) was gone out into the middle of the court, the Lord bade him turn again with contrary message, and told Hezekiah that he had heard his prayer (even that uncomfortable prayer) and seen his tears and healed him. So, as within three days he should be able to go up into the house of the Lord, yes, that he would also add to his days 15 years, (2 Kings 20:4-5). David felt a small sweetness in the prayer he made at that time, when he said in his haste, he was but a cast-away; but even that prayer was a sweet odor to God, as appears by the comfortable answer he received from God even at that time. Psalm 31:22, "Though I said in my haste I am cast out of thy sight, yet thou heardest the voice of my prayer when I cryed unto thee."

Will God so respect the prayers that his poor servants make to him in spirit and in truth, even when their hearts are so oppressed with grief that they cannot pray with any cheerfulness? Yes, then, when (in affliction of mind) they have so far forth yielded to their infidelity, as that they doubt they are no better than hypocrites, and reprobates, that he desires even then such prayers. He would have them even when they are in that case to pray to him, yes, he delights and takes pleasure even in such prayers. Then is this most true, which our Savior here teaches us, that the Father even seeks and desires such worshippers as can worship him in spirit and in truth, though they do it weakly and imperfectly.

3. Yet will the force of this reason better appear if we consider the third point. It is, how the Lord stands affected to that worship which hypocrites do to him, that worship him only in ceremony, not in spirit and in truth.

1. He does not regard such service men do to him, nor takes any pleasure in it. Isaiah 1:11, "What have I to do with the multitude of your sacrifices?" This is as if he

should say, "What do I care about them? Gen. 4:5, "Unto
Cain and to his offering the Lord had no respect." No not
when they pray to him with the most devotion and
earnestness, as in their extreme affliction, yet the Lord
does not regard it, no more then you regard the roaring of
the bear or bull when they are baited. This the hypocrites
complain of, "Wherefore have we fasted and thou seest
not? Wherefore have we afflicted our soul and thou
takest no knowledge?" (Isaiah 58:3). And in this way the
Lord threatens, "I also will laugh at your calamity; I will
mock when your fear cometh; when your fear cometh as
desolation, and your destruction cometh as a whirlwind;
when distress and anguish cometh upon you. Then shall
they call upon me, but I will not answer; they shall seek
me early, but they shall not find me," (Prov. 1:26-28).
Though such a man offer the very same service to God,
that the Lord has in his word commanded, though he says
good prayers, hears the word sincerely taught, receives
the sacraments sincerely administered, he loses all his
labor he has done because he does it without being
thankful. This is because God desires no such matter at
their hands. Psalm 50:16, "Unto the wicked," God says,
"what cause hast thou to do to declare my statutes, or
that thou shouldest take my covenant in thy mouth?" As
if he should say, "Why have you offered this kind of
service to God?" Therefore, it is added in that place of
Isaiah 1:12, "Who required this at your hands to tread in
my courts?" As if he should say, it is more fit for you to be
in your shops, or in the ale-house, or anywhere else then
here. Psalm 118:20, "This is the gate of the Lord, the
righteous shall enter into it." Many others come in that
are not righteous, nor have so much as a desire to be

godly, or purpose to leave their sins. But these people hate those that are godly with all their hearts. Here the Lord takes no pleasure to see such, but askes them, who gave them authority to come here? It is not so dangerous a presumption (I assure you) for a rogue that has the infection of the plague running in him to press into the King's private chamber, and there to offer to wait at his table, as much as it is for the drunkard, whoremonger, swearer and hater of godliness to come into God's house, or to take on him to offer God any service. Make a note how the Lord casts this in the teeth of ungodly men. Jer. 7:9-11, "Will you steal and commit adultery, and swear, and come and stand before me in this house, whereupon my name is called. Is this house become a den of thieves (or a receptacle for whores and adulterers, for swearers and drunkards) behold even I see it, saith the Lord."

2. God does not desire their service, but rejects it. Isaiah 1:11, "I desire not the blood of bullocks, nor of lambs, nor of goats?" No, did not the Lord himself require and command these sacrifices? Yes, to his people, those who were true worshippers, he did; but not to the hypocrite and wicked man.

3. He abhors the best service they can do to him, and detests them, even for praying to him, and taking upon them to offer him service. Isaiah 1:13, "Incense is an abomination to me, I cannot suffer your new moons, nor sabbaths, my soul hateth your new moons, they are a burden to me, I am weary to bear them." It is a thing the Lord abhors, and hates to see a wicked man use prayer, or frequent church assemblies in this way. A strange and fearful, yet a most true saying, make note on this that I bring before you, in Prov. 21:27, "The sacrifice of the

wicked is an abomination," how much more is it when he brings it with a wicked heart? As if he should say, "Though he does not mean ill in it, but has a good meaning in it to serve God, yet it is an abomination to the Lord.

Some will object to this, and if any shall say this is strange doctrine, if we are never so bad, would you not have us come to church, would you not have us pray, and serve God? Many a bad man has received much good by coming to church, so they will say.

I answer, 1. God indeed has commanded all men to serve him. The Moral Law was given to Adam and all his posterity. Wicked men shall be damned because they have not prayed and heard his word. Yes, it shall be easier in the day of judgement for that wicked man that has used these things to try and to serve God, then for him that is utterly irreligious and profane. Therefore, the Lord condemns the very atheist because he did not pray, (Psalm 14:4).

2. The wicked by this service to God often obtains freedom from temporal judgements that otherwise would fall on him. In this he gets temporal rewards, (1 Kings 21:29), as Ahab did so.

3. Many a wicked man by coming into God's house, (yes, even when he has come with a wicked intent) have been effectually called, as the unbeliever that Paul speaks of in 1 Cor. 14:25-26. And this applies to those messengers that were sent to apprehend Christ in John 7:46. In which three respects, it may be thought good policy for the wicked man to pray, and hear the word, and to serve God.

4. No sin that any man has lived in, in former times, can make his prayers or service ever a bit the less acceptable to God if he now repents. The publican on his unfeigned humiliation and repentance went home justified, (Luke 18:13-14). So that this *doctrine* does not push people to the terror and discomfort of any the most notorious sinners that is penitent; but to the impenitent sinner, to the man that continues in sin, it is indeed a fearful doctrine (and if it is not fearful now being uttered by a weak man, yet it will certainly be fearful to you when the Lord shall charge it on your conscience). God does not regard any service you do to him, no, he would not have you offer him any service, no, he *abhors* whatever service comes from you in this way.

CHAPTER 12:
WORSHIP IN SPIRIT

I have finished the first reason that our Savior here brings to confirm this doctrine. His second reason is this, that "God is a Spirit." Now in this second reason we must consider, first the meaning of the words, then the force they have to conclude that for which Christ alleges in them.

First then we must not take these words as a perfect definition of the nature of God. For that which is here spoken of God, agrees also to the angels, and to the soul of a man. The angels are spirits, "Who maketh his angels spirits; his ministers a flaming fire," (Psalm 104:4). "Are they not all ministering spirits, sent forth to minister for them who shall be heirs of salvation?" (Heb. 1:14). The soul of man also is a spirit. Eccl. 12:7, "The spirit shall return to God who gave it. "And they stoned Stephen, calling upon God, and saying, Lord Jesus, receive my spirit," (Acts 7:59). But because of all the creatures God has made, these do most fully and lively resemble the divine nature. It has pleased the Lord (having respect in this to the weakness and shallowness of our capacity) to call himself a *Spirit* both here, and in other places of holy Scripture. 2 Cor. 3:17, "The Lord is a Spirit." Heb. 9:14, Christ's God-head is called "the eternal Spirit." 1. As they are immortal, so the Lord is immortal, yes, but only he has immortality (1 Tim. 6:16) of himself. 2. As they are wise and understanding natures, so the Lord is of himself infinite in wisdom. In which respect he is called "God only wise," (1 Tim. 1:17). 3. As they are simple, invisible, incorporeal, not having mixture, nor consisting of any corporeal substance. And therefore Christ proves himself after his resurrection, not to be a spirit by this reason, "Behold my hands and my feet, that it is I myself: handle me, and see; for a spirit hath not flesh and bones, as ye see me have," (Luke 24:39); so is the Lord. And in this respect principally is the Lord called a Spirit in this place, because he does not have a visible, sensible, corporal nature, but he is of a spiritual nature.

Now for the force that is in this reason to conclude that for which Christ brings it, is that true worshippers must worship the Father in spirit and truth, not with a ceremonial and outward worship, *because God is a Spirit.* The force (I say) of this reason is evident. His worship must be answerable to his own nature. Such as he is, such must the worshippers be that he delights in. According to the proverb, *like* will have *like;* like master, like man. Such as a man's own disposition is, such he desires they should be that serve him. David had no better an argument to prove that he did unfeignedly fear God then this, that all his delight was in godly men, (Psalm 16:3). Specially that his care was to seek out such to serve him as feared God. Psalm 101:1, "Mine eyes shall be to the faithful in the land, that they may dwell with me, he that walketh in a perfect way, he shall serve me." This reason the Lord often uses. Lev. 19:2, "Ye shall be holy, for I the Lord your God am holy." As if he should say: *because you are my servants, my people, you must frame yourselves to my disposition, and seek to be like me.* The Lord, therefore, being a Spirit himself, sets his eye on the spirit and heart of man, to see how he is served there. 1 Samuel 16:7, "The Lord looketh not as a man looketh: for man looketh on the outward appearance, but the Lord looketh on the heart." His delight is to have service done to him with the spirit and heart. "Behold thou desirest truth in the inward parts," David says in Psalm 51:6. Let the adorning of a Christian, the Apostle says in 1 Peter 3:4, "be the hidden man of the heart in that which is not corruptible, even the ornament of a meek and quiet spirit, which is in the sight of God of great price." So that he that thinks a ceremonial and bodily worship will make the Lord content, judges erroneously of his nature, and indeed makes an idol and a false god of him.

But it may be objected, that there seems to be no consequence in this *reason*, the true worshippers must now after Christ's ascension worship God in a more spiritual manner then they have done under the Law, because God is a Spirit. Why? God was a Spirit then as well as now.

To this I answer, that it is true indeed, and therefore he always required to be worshipped in spirit, for even to them under the Law it was said in Deuteronomy 10:16, "Circumcise the fore-skin of your hearts." Hosea 6:6, "I desired mercy and not sacrifice, and the knowledge of God more then burnt offerings." But as the Lord has more clearly revealed himself now to be a spirit, to be of a spiritual nature more then he did under the Law, so he requires the spiritual worship of his people now more then he did under the Law. Then God revealed himself to his people in many sensible apparitions, visions, and voices, having respect in that time to the infirmity of his church, while she was in her child-hood. We know the Lord appeared to Abraham in the body of a man, and talked familiarly with him, as one friend does with another, (Gen. 18:28). And in a vision to Ezekiel he appeared in the similitude of a man sitting on a throne, (Ezek. 1:26). So, with an audible and sensible voice, he delivered the Law to his people in Deut. 5:26. In a sensible and visible manner he guided his people through the wilderness in a pillar of cloud by day, and a pillar of fire by night, (Exod. 13:51). By a sensible and material fire that came down from heaven, he witnessed often-times his approbation of the sacrifices that his servants offered to him, (1 Cor. 21:26). In a sensible and visible manner, his glory filled both the tabernacle and the temple, (2 Chron. 7:2).

Now since the days of Christ, the Lord has not been accustomed to reveal himself to his church in this corporal and sensible manner, but as he is a spirit, so in a spiritual manner he only has revealed himself to his church. It is therefore spoken of as a blessing peculiar to the days under the Gospel, that on all sorts of his people, he will pour his spirit in a far more plentiful manner, then ever he had done before, (Joel 2:28-29).

Having now finished the *doctrine* that our Savior delivers in these two verses, and both of the reasons that he brings for its confirmation, it remains that we make our *use* of it.

The first use of it is to condemn the religion of the Papists. If we had no other reason against Popery, this would be sufficient to prove it as false worship, such as God does not allow, because it in every way matches, yes, far exceeds the form of worship that was under the Law; even in that point, for which our Savior here condemns it. The vestments their priests use in God's service, the church-music and many other things are used in imitation of the Jews. But 1. In observation of days and times, in the number of their holy days: 2. In the multitude of their significant ceremonies: 3. In the pomp and worldly stateliness of their prelates and clergy: 4. In their superstitious ringing, and set service, and other ceremonies about burial: they far exceed the Jews.

If that form of worship which God himself appointed under the Law, must necessarily be abrogated as Christ has here taught us, and no true worshipper might use it any longer because it stood so much in external and carnal rites in shadows, and significant ceremonies, then certainly those that use and delight in such a kind of worship that was devised by men must necessarily be deemed hypocrites and false worshippers of God. See the judgement that our Savior gives of these kinds of ceremonies, and of those that are addicted to them. The Jews in his time had a ceremony that they would not eat meat before they had washed often, holding the tradition of the elders, (Mark 7:3). This might as lawfully have been used as any religious ceremony that was devised by man. For, it was not used in God's service, and might have seemed to be but a civil ceremony. Yet our Savior discerns that it was enjoined by the elders, and was observed by the Jews as a significant ceremony, a doctrine to the conscience, a means to put it into a kind of spiritual duty, (Mark 7:7). It was a thing in which they put holiness, and which they accounted as a worthy service done to God. Jesus would not use it himself, (Luke 11:38), and taught his disciples to refuse it, and defended them for so doing, (Mark 7:6). And this he did though he saw it would provoke the Pharisees greatly, and be likely to draw him and his disciples into trouble, (Mark 7:3). And he gives three reasons against them. 1. He makes it a certain note of a hypocrite (of a carnal man that has no soundness of grace in him) to be addicted to these ceremonies, (Mark 7:6). In which respect also (among others) the ceremonial Law is called a carnal commandment, (Heb. 7:16), and the rudiments of the world, (Gal. 4:3). 2. That it is vain worship, (Mark 7:7). There is no profit nor sound edification that can come to the conscience by it. The Apostle therefore calls the ceremonies, impotent and beggarly rudiments, (Gal. 4:9). Observe it well where they are used with most conscience and devotion (as in Popery they are) they work no knowledge or sanctification in men. 3. That where they are used, they will make the commandments of God of no authority, (Matt. 15:6). They will destroy the power of true piety and godliness, and even eat out its heart. And that was the cause why Satan did not labor in anything more busily in the primitive church then to bring in again the ceremonial worship, after God had abrogated it, and the Apostle calls them that were his instruments in this work, dogs; that is, "enemies to all piety," (Phil. 3:2).

The second use of the doctrine comes more to concern ourselves. It teaches us to take heed of hypocrisy in the service of God. Strive to worship him in spirit and truth. Luke 12:1, "Take heed to yourselves (our Savior says) of the leaven of the Pharisees which is hypocrisy." The Lord exceedingly abhors hypocrisy in his service. The more service you offer to God, the more you provoke him if you are a hypocrite. "But the hypocrites in heart heap up wrath: they cry not when he bindeth them," (Job.

36:13). For the hypocrite is a false worshipper; he makes an idol of God; he thinks he can deceive God as he does men.

Now there are three kinds and degrees of hypocrites that worship God in some other way than in spirit and truth, and are therefore called here by Christ, false worshippers of God.

1. They that do any service to God only with their bodies, without the understanding, feeling and devotion of the heart. In every service we offer to God he still calls for the heart. "My son give me thy heart" he says, (Prov. 23:26). Paul had not pleased God in preaching, if he had not in preaching served God in his spirit, (Romans 1:9). Lydia had not pleased God in hearing the word, if her heart had not been opened; if she had not heard with feeling and affection of heart, (Acts 16:14). No man can please God in praying to him, unless he prays with the feeling and affection of his spirit. Psalm 86:4, "Rejoice the soul of thy servant, for unto the Lord do I lift up my soul." Nor can this be in singing of Psalms unless he sings with grace in his heart to the Lord, (Eph. 5:19). Our prayers are compared to odors, (Rev. 5:8), and to incense, (Psalm 141:2), and the fervency of our affection is as the fire without which these odors and incense can never send up any sweet savor to God. In this respect the Apostle bids us to be fervent in spirit as serving the Lord, (Romans 12:11), as if no service could be acceptable to God without frequency of spirit. Let every one of us therefore have a principal care of what, both in our prayers, and in every other part of the worship we do to God.

Two good helps are needful to be used to this purpose: 1. Watchfulness, for we must continue in prayer and watch in the same. "Continue in prayer, and watch in the same with thanksgiving," (Col. 4:2), for unless we have an eye to this, and watch our hearts well, they will be roving. And as this is needful in all our prayers, so especially in prescript and set forms of prayer, which we have often accustomed ourselves to. 2. To set ourselves as in God's presence, and bring our hearts to a reverent fear of God's majesty before whom we appear. "Serve the Lord with fear," (Psalm 2:11). "In thy fear will I worship toward thine holy temple," (Psalm 5:7).

The second sort of hypocrites that do not worship God in spirit and truth, are they that use God's worship or any part of it, as a matter of ceremony and formality only, and never seek in it, the edification of the spirit and conscience. 1. That preacher is but a hypocrite that seeks not so to preach, as his preaching may have power in the hearts of his hearers. "But I will come to you shortly, if the Lord will, and will know, not the speech of them which are puffed up, but the power. For the kingdom of God is not in word, but in power," (1 Cor. 4:19-20). And he makes this a note of an able minister of the Gospel when he is the minister of the spirit, (2 Cor. 3:6). It is that which we should seek to see God's seal on our ministry in the hearts of our hearers, "the seal of mine Apostleship are ye in the Lord," yes, he says this was his main answer and defense to those that examined him and questioned his ministry, (1 Cor. 9:2). 3. We have need not only to preach, but to teach such *doctrine* as is profitable, and which particularly concerns, and is of use to those we teach. This was Paul's direction to Titus, to teach and stand on those things in his ministry that were good and profitable to men, (Titus 3:8). Neither only to teach, but to use application also, "Preach the word, reprove, or convince, rebuke, exhort," (2 Tim. 4:2).

Those Christians are no better than hypocrites, who (so they have a form of God's service) never care whether it edifies their conscience or not in such worship. Such are they as rest content with a dumb ministry, for what power do they feel in it? Such also are they as hear good preachers, and praise them, but never examine what profit they receive in their conscience by them. When you praise a good preacher (whose ministry you frequent) with your tongue, your life, and *unreformed course* this disgraces him. Those hearers only praise their teachers indeed that have profited in reformation of heart and life by their ministry; in whose hearts the spirit of God has written that of their minister's commendation, as may be read of all men, (2 Cor. 3:2).

3. The third sort of hypocrites that do not worship God in spirit and truth, are they that will be devout in the exercises of religion, and zealous in profession, "Make a show of godliness," but deny its power, (2 Tim. 3:5). True religion where it is received, will command the heart and the whole man. Let a man profess what he will, if his heart and life is not reformed, he is a hypocrite; and whatever worship he does to God is but a false worship. We know that God does not hear sinners, but if any man be a worshipper of God, and does his will, him he hears, (John 9:31), Yes, the very service he offers to God increases God's wrath against him. You must either amend your life, or give up serving God.

FINIS

OTHER WORKS ON WORSHIP BY PURITAN PUBLICATIONS

Vain Imaginations in the Worship of God by Jonathan Edwards et al.

The Simplicity of Holy Worship by John Wilson (1588–1667)

The Glory of Evangelical Worship by John Owen (1616-1683)

A Christian's True Spiritual Worship to Jesus Christ by Stephen Charnock (1628-1680)

True Worship and the Consequences of Idolatry by John Knox (1505-1572)

Gospel Worship, or, The Right Manner of Sanctifying the name of God in General, in Hearing the word, Receiving the Lord's Supper, and Prayer by Jeremiah Burroughs (1599-1646)

How to Serve God in Private and Public Worship by John Jackson (1600-1648)

The Christian's Charge Never to Offend God in Worship by John Forbes (1568-1634)

A Biblical Response to Superstition, Will-Worship and the Christmas Holiday by Daniel Cawdrey (1588-1664)

The Use of Instruments of Music in Christian Corporate Worship Indefensible by James Begg, D.D.